Manifesting Wealth
Magic for Prosperity, Love, and Health

Manifesting Wealth
Magic for Prosperity, Love, and Health

Taylor Ellwood

Megalithica Books

Stafford England

ManifestingWealth: Magic for Prosperity, Love, and Health
by Taylor Ellwood
© 2014 First edition

Cover Art: Andy Bigwood
Editor: Kat Bailey
Layout: Taylor Ellwood http://www.magicalexperiments.com

Set in Poor Richard and Book Antiqua

MB0166

ISBN 9781905713929

Megalithica Books Edition 2014

A Megalithica Books Publication
An imprint of Immanion Press
http://www.immanion-press.com
info@immanion-press.com

Table of Contents

Dedication

To Kelson and Kyra, in the hope that both of you will live lives of health, wealth, love, and happiness!

Acknowledgements

First and foremost, I want to acknowledge Kat, whose unconditional belief in me and love for me has become a source of strength for me. She makes me feel wealthy every day. I also want to acknowledge Storm Constantine, and the rest of Immanion Press. A better team of people couldn't be asked for in publishing. A special thanks goes to Crystal Blanton, for writing the introduction of this book and for all the work she does in general. Finally, my thanks to the people who follow magical experiments and read my books. The support I've heard in the last couple of years has truly been heartwarming.

Foreword

I've occasionally struggled as I've written this book, wondering if I'm really someone who should be writing a book on wealth magic. The reason for that occasional struggle is that I don't fit the classic definition of wealth. I am not a multi-million or billionaire with lots of money. In fact I am a self-employed business owner who currently has some debt, some money for retirement, and who has some financial strategies, which include magic, that are helping me to make my life into a reality of wealth. However I don't think that wealth is just determined by how financially savvy a person is.

It seems to me that wealth is partially based on a person's skills with finances, but also on a person's skills with relationships (both personal and professional), skills with whatever form of work s/he takes on, and his/her ability to take care of health needs (both physical and mental). This is admittedly not the typical definition of wealth, but the typical definition of wealth is one that seems to be far out of reach for most people, and may not even be accurately called wealth (as I'll explore later).

Whenever the topic of wealth magic is brought up, what fascinates me is how people treat the topic. There is an expectation that if you are able to do wealth magic, you should be fantastically rich and successful. Indeed, it might be argued that if you can't display such evidence of material wealth then you shouldn't write on the topic. Yet I can't say that I know any occultist who is fantastically rich. I do, however, know some occultists who have gotten their financial ducks in a row, live a relatively stable life and have a plan for retirement. That's not necessarily as glamorous as a wealthy lifestyle, but a look through any tabloid suggests that while someone may be rich, they are not necessarily wealthy. Imagine never being able to go out into public without being ambushed by paparazzi or always having to wear a disguise? Imagine wondering whether someone was really your friend or just wanted to be associated with you for your fame? Of course not every rich person is famous, but I imagine that being rich is not necessarily all it's cracked up to be.

So what then really is wealth? In this book, I explore the topic of wealth from a holistic perspective, which means that while I do focus on financial magic and strategies that can improve your relationship with money, I also look at other facets of your life such as health and relationships. I think that an accurate snapshot of wealth necessarily needs to encompass more than just doing a money spell to get more money. And while I think that money can make your life easier, it is not guaranteed to make you happy. Money is a tool and knowing how to use that tool wisely can make your life much happier. Understanding that distinction is important if you want to master wealth magic and use it effectively to enhance your life.

I admitted above that I've had some debt. I've had periods of my life where I didn't have debt, but one of the problems that I have with most wealth magic books is that the authors don't present their mistakes or the struggles they are facing. Of course this may be due to the fact that they want to present a certain image of authority or show how successful they are. But if we consider the role of magic in our lives, it is not all glamour and spells. It is a way of life, a way of perspective and observation that teaches us how to solve problems while also living a better life. That can't occur if we don't show how we've struggled, or what we've learned.

I present to you this book in the hopes that you will learn how to create a wealthier life for yourself, but I also present it to show you how someone has gotten some success, but also made some mistakes along the way. I am certainly not the wealthiest magician financially, but I have learned some financial tricks and tips through the years, and I am wealthy in other ways that have helped me improve all aspects of my life. I share my journey and my approaches to wealth magic so that you can learn from them and find success and happiness in your life. Those experiences are truly what makes a person wealthy!

Taylor Ellwood
Portland, OR
May 2013

Introduction by Crystal Blanton

The concept of wealth is often reduced to a one-dimensional concept of happiness that is directly tied to money. This capitalistic ideal of American wealth leaves very little room for a definition that matches the multidimensional layers of a person's life. Money is not the only tool that is needed for a person to achieve a level of wealth that increases opportunities to thrive, and live a balanced and enriched life.

And while American values encapsulate an egalitarian concept of opportunity for wealth, many of us struggle to understand what it means to have wealth and how to get it. Many of us do not understand that wealth often is a frame of mind, and not a dollar figure inside of a bank account. Attainable measures of wealth are not limited to money, and often come with the limitless opportunities to find fulfillment spiritually, physically, mentally, and financially.

Manifesting Wealth: Magic for Prosperity, Love, and Health gives readers information that will take them from concept, to the reality of embracing wealth, to improve their quality of life. Taylor Ellwood has created a book that is full of ideas and information, pushing the reader beyond old ideals of wealth, to a more holistic sense of possessing great personal wealth.

Taylor captures definitions that are inclusive of all people by allowing different measurements to what wealth really is. Not everyone can be "rollin" in the dough, but everyone is capable of attaining wealth. Taylor defines this concept by stating, "Wealth is the measurement of the quality of a person's life, as well as a measurement of how that person sustains the specific lifestyle that brings him/her the most joy".

He goes on to further define that wealth is based on the "quality of experiences that you have, as opposed to the quantity of things you've acquired. As such, living a life of wealth doesn't necessarily involve having lots of money, but rather involves knowing how to make your resources work for you so that you can focus on living your life and pursuing your calling".

There is an emphasis in the book on definitions, planning,

and internal work to achieve ones defined goals. There are also exercises that are placed throughout the chapters, meant to make the reader think, plot and plan for success in wealth. The book explores how a person's ability to obtain wealth will directly connect to the relationship one has with money, and the values that have been conditioned on limiting beliefs about how money relates to life. The messages that become a part of our unconscious schema often involve money as a link to happiness, and who is or is not deserving of this.

Taylor talks about the relationships that we cultivate with happiness, money, and worth, as they are directly tied to how we were taught by our parents. It is what we saw, or didn't see, that helped to formulate a relationship with the concept of wealth that can become a person's greatest challenges to acquiring a true understanding of abundance.

I appreciated this aspect on attaining wealth from the book because it is a limiting belief that I have unconsciously carried about the value of my work for years, and how doing work in the community does not equal a life of monetary abundance. While other service workers like myself are paid in love, financially I learned from my mother at a young age that when you give yourself to the work of people, you do not do it to get rich.

And so I have found, that 16 years in the social services field has afforded me an incredible career on a very middle to lower class salary. And this is where Taylor's lessons of creating a wealth identity becomes magical.

Do your current values, beliefs and persona encourage, and motivate, you to bring wealth into your life? Are you open to the potential of your life, and are you open to the possibilities that it is within your reach to have those things that bring you joy? These are all questions that are raised in this book that I could not answer for myself. I was not raised to have those limitless beliefs, and as a Witch, I know that my beliefs very much shape manifestation.

I enjoyed that the book continues into discussions of magical elements of working with money, identifying money deities, wealth entities, and money altars. It doesn't stop there and also gives specific information about working within a business, or to call advancement to you in your current job. The amount of information that is broken down in the book gives a solid understanding of acquiring wealth from a foundation of magic, values, perspective, and by having a plan. Both the magical and the mundane workings of calling abundance to you are addressed, making it more than a simple book on doing a money spell.

And it doesn't stop there. Taylor explores wealth and its relationship to physical health, mental healthy, spiritual health, relationships, and community. He continues to make connections between the whole of our being, and our ability to embrace wealth from a holistic view. By making these connections, the book continues to point out how enjoying wealth is a direct part of encompassing the ability to have it.

As a social worker and a mental health professional, I appreciate the inclusion of the whole person in discussions about the ability to bring joy into one's life, and attribute that to the idea of being wealthy. Opening up the definition of wealth beyond money gives more opportunity for people to connect to, and understand that, they can have what will enrich their journey and improve their quality of life. The more that people are given the power to be in control of creating a happy and enriched life, the more people will chose to do just that.

May we all grab opportunity before us, and bring layers of abundance and wealth into our lives. I hope this book is another step in that exact journey for you too.

Crystal Blanton
December 2013

Chapter 1: What's Your Definition of Wealth?

This isn't your typical wealth magic book. This is a holistic wealth magic book, which means that we'll look at wealth from a holistic perspective that encompasses your entire life, as opposed to just focusing on how much money you are bringing in. We will focus on your relationship with money, what it looks like, and what you can do to change it. At the same time, it's worth noting that too many people define wealth solely by money without really understanding that money is just one means and medium among many of attaining wealth. Money is powerful in its own way (look at how many conflicts, inventions, etc., are motivated by money or some other form of material wealth) and it does have a place in this book, but defining wealth solely by monetary value ignores what wealth really is, or what it could be. At the same time, assigning a monetary value to wealth can help you determine if you are actually achieving the wealth you want to generate in your life. As I tell my business clients, "If you can't track where the money is flowing from, you don't where your business is going to!" I think that's true not just for business, but also for life. So money has a role in wealth and we won't ignore it, but I think to really understand wealth, it's important to understand that money is only part of the equation. Your friends, romantic partner(s), health, and quality of life are equally a part of wealth, and to do effective wealth magic, we need to look at the whole picture of your life.

To understand wealth you need to define it. More importantly though, you need to define it in relationship to your identity. Wealth is a fairly nebulous term and can mean a lot of different things to many different people. Wealth is also associated with being rich. Here's one definition of being rich that's also linked to wealth:

> The person who owns all he wants for the living of all life he is capable of living is rich. Nobody can have all he wants without plenty of money. Life has advanced so far and become so complex

that even the most ordinary man or woman requires a great amount of wealth in order to live in a manner that even approaches completeness. Every person naturally wants to become all he is capable of becoming; this desire to realize innate possibilities is inherent in human nature. Success in life is becoming what you want to be" (Wattles 2007, p.4).

The author originally wrote that quote in 1910, over a hundred years ago, but it's fairly clear that he links wealth to being rich and argues that true success is linked to having whatever you want. When you read that definition do you get a kneejerk reaction or do you agree with it? Regardless of what response you have, take a moment to write it down and explore why you have that response.

Wattles says, "No person can rise to his greatest possible height in talent or soul development unless he has plenty of money. In order to unfold the soul and to develop talent he must have many things to use, and he cannot have all these things unless he has money to buy them with" (Wattles 2007, P. 3). While I think he makes an interesting point, I can't help but disagree, especially when you consider the vast majority of celebrities, rich people, etc., all of whom have plenty of money, but nonetheless don't seem to live very fulfilling lives. Money alone doesn't guarantee a happy, or satisfied life. It certainly helps to attain things, but the commodization of our lives isn't something that brings a lot of happiness. In fact, the more that people value and focus on material aspirations, the less happy they are with their lives (Kassar 2006) Genuine satisfaction doesn't arise because you have money and can buy things. Genuine satisfaction occurs because you are living life by your own rules.

One of the key criteria of wealth is the concept of success. The following definition of success is one that reminds me of magical work, "Success is an attitude. Success is a habit. Success is easily available to all who want it, *believe* they can have it, and put their desires into action [italics are his]" (Fisher & Allen 2008, P. 1). That last sentence could easily describe a magical act. A given result is available to all who want it, believe they can have it, and put their desires into action. If we consider that magic is a methodology used to manifest specific results that improve the quality of one's life, then this could work, but there's more to success or wealth than just manifesting a result. We also need to create a sustainable process that allows us to not only manifest wealth, but to consistently live a life where we can maintain that wealth, even as it in turn maintains us.

To illustrate that principle, let's consider the lottery. The lottery is a game of chance people play in order to potentially win up to millions of dollars. But the majority of lottery winners end up spending the money they won and end up more miserable as well because they were hit up by relatives and friends for loans. Most importantly they didn't know what to do with all that money (Gardner and Gardner, 2001). The reason they didn't know is simple: They shot for a specific result (win millions of dollars), but they didn't think about what to do with it afterwards. They didn't develop a sustainable strategy for how they would invest that money or use it, or consider how it would impact their lives. The whole point of wealth is to create a sustainable lifestyle that supports you. Having lots of money does not equate to having a sustainable lifestyle. Knowing how to use your money to improve the quality of your life and sustain it is much more important than the quantity of money you have available to you (Gardner & Gardner 2001, Dominguez and Robin 1992). Many people think that if they just have x amount of money life will be much easier, but that rarely seems to be the case. If anything, people spend more time worrying about money than actually enjoying it. And once they make x amount of money they find that they need more money and go back into daydreaming about how life would be perfect if they just had more money!

There are three problems that pervade Western culture, when it comes to money. The first problem is rampant consumerism and the obsession to have stuff. This rampant consumerism puts people into debt and leaves them with things that aren't even used that often. Hoarding is an extreme version of this consumerism and is driven in part by the dysfunctional relationship a person has with money. It's as if people are trying to fill something up within themselves (an internal emptiness), with stuff. And perhaps they are. The problem is that stuff can't fill that internal emptiness. If anything, stuff only emphasizes how empty your life is, especially if you can't meaningfully use it to make your life better.

The second problem is the focus on the law of attraction as espoused most recently by such new agey claptrap as *The Secret*. The law of attraction argues that if you think positive thoughts you will get positive outcomes, and if you think negative thoughts you will get negative outcomes. While there is some truth to this idea, it can be taken to an extreme such as believing that if you open an envelope while having positive thoughts you are more likely to get a positive outcome, and if you open it with negative thoughts you are more likely to have a negative outcome. Additionally this law explains away issues such as obesity with the idea the person must be attracting that obesity with their thoughts, when in fact the person may just be genetically predisposed toward obesity. The law of attraction was made popular by the movie *The Secret*, but the concept has been around much longer. Napoleon Hill and Wallace Wattles both wrote books espousing similar ideas, and in one form or another you find it in books that focus on trying to teach people how to become millionaires. While it would be nice to believe that thinking about wealth alone could attract positive results, the truth is that the law of attraction is a pipe dream. After all, how do you explain the vast amount of hunger, poverty, or the economic recession? Are all of those people simply thinking they are poor and causing their own misfortune? The answer is no. The idea that thought alone can generate negative consequences makes dangerous assumptions that further increase the gap between the haves and the have nots.

This isn't to say that thinking positively doesn't have any value. It does have value and can be useful for helping you be more creative, as well as finding solutions in negative situations. But thinking positively doesn't guarantee that you'll be a multi-millionaire or that you'll never deal with negative situations. Thinking positively is helpful, and we'll explore how to use it in your magical working, but there is a difference between positive thinking and the idea that thinking you are wealthy will automatically bring you wealth.

The third problem is that people simply don't know what to do with money or understand how it applies to wealth. So you have people who desperately pursue money for money's sake while others ignorantly believe that money is the root of all evil. What both types of people have forgotten, or never learned, is that money is just a tool, a means to an end. It is not the root of evil, but pursuing money as an end in and of itself never works. If you do not understand how to use money, then no matter how much you have you are a slave to it. This is why there are rich people who have a lot of money, but aren't wealthy. They are so focused on acquiring money that they don't do know what else to do with it, or how to use it to enrich their lives. This is also why you have celebrities who are in debt despite making lots of money. They may seem wealthy, but if anything, they are struggling just as much as the average person is because they don't know how to handle money wisely. Simply having a lot of money doesn't make you wealthy.

Exercise

Which of these three problems (if any) apply to your relationship with money? How has money shown up in your life in a positive or negative way?

If the first problem, consumerism, applies to you, meditate on why you are always buying something and what you are trying to accomplish by buying so much stuff. Does the stuff really make you happy or does it just disguise a deeper issue you need to work with?

If the second problem, Law of Attraction thinking, applies to you, meditate on the law and what you've attracted to your life. Are you really responsible for every misfortune you've experienced? Could you control every aspect of your reality? How are you applying action to achieve what you want to attract in your life?

If the third problem, not knowing what to do with money, applies to you, meditate on your relationship with money. Where did you learn your financial skills? Who or what taught you your current financial habits? What would you change about your relationship with money, if you could change one thing?

Write down your experiences, and after a day has passed read them over. What actions can you take to change your relationship with money and yourself?
Jason Miller notes that a lot of people have reactive attitudes and thoughts when it comes to money. If everything is okay, they don't want to think about money or engage it. He also notes that typical financial magic focuses on providing a person enough money so that s/he doesn't have to think about it (2012). I agree with Miller's assessment of financial magic and the attitude put toward it. People do magic to get just enough money to resolve whatever crisis or problem is in their life, or so they don't have to think about money. Yet ironically, they end up thinking about money all the time. It seems contradictory to me, and I think it's one reason so much money magic fails. If you don't want to think about it, or how it applies to your life, what you are really telling the universe is that you don't want money. The universe is always happy to oblige.

There is a solution to all of these problems: that solution is developing a plan for your life that includes actions you will take to realize that plan. The most successful people are not the ones who have had lots of positive thoughts (although positive thinking may be part of what they use), but rather the ones who have planned for the success they want to achieve and then implemented that plan through action and adaptation to events. They've also realized that success doesn't always involve making tons of money. What it really involves is living life on your own terms. Part of accomplishing that involves getting clear on your relationship with money and how you are blocking yourself with your beliefs about money.

So What is Wealth?

One of my favorite financial books is *Your Money or Your Life* by Joe Dominguez and Vicki Robin. In that book the authors spend a lot of time discussing the quality of a person's life and why the quality of your life is so essential to living a wealthy life. If there is one book (other than this one) that you should pick up, it's that book. Wealth is the measurement of the quality of a person's life, as well as a measurement of how that person sustains the specific lifestyle that brings him/her the most joy. That definition is derived from the aforementioned book, which provides cases studies of many people who live a life of financial independence despite not being "dyed in the wool" multi-millionaires. What they've learned to do is to leverage their money into investments while also cutting down the cost of living so that they can focus on living a life of quality doing what they feel called to do.

I define wealth as the means a person has available to support and sustain his/her chosen lifestyle while also allowing that person to pursue the career/business that s/he feels called to do. Wealth is based on the quality of experiences that you have as opposed to the quantity of things you've acquired. As such, living a life of wealth doesn't necessarily involve having lots of money, but rather involves knowing how to make your resources work for you so that you can focus on living your life and pursuing your calling. Money, as it pertains to wealth, is a means to an end, specifically money is a tool used to support your life, and not just in terms of paying bills, but also making investments that in turn produce dividends that can be used to support you. Money is just one means to supporting yourself and finding wealth. There are other means such as bartering and growing your own resources. Wealth is also discovered in the quality of relationships you have with other people and with your sense of place in the world at large. Dave Lee points out that, "Wealth is an attitude to life which is always with you, and the nature of wealth magick is the acquisition of wealth consciousness. Wealth consciousness is the organize belief in the inevitability of for you" (2011 P. 59). I agree with Lee that wealth is an attitude. Wealth magic is the application of that attitude to your life.

Wealth magic is magic that is done to help you achieve wealth. It can involve money magic, but it can just as easily involve doing magic to help you discover your true calling. The point of wealth magic is that it helps you improve your relationship with how you sustain your lifestyle, while also helping you discover and use your calling to aid in supporting your lifestyle.

Exercise

What is your definition of wealth? Where does money fit into that definition? What other means do you use to support yourself and bring joy into your life? If your definition of wealth is different of mine, why is it different, and what makes that definition of wealth work for you? Most importantly, does your wealth bring you joy?

I use the word joy in relationship to wealth, because I think that having a sense of joy is as important as having wealth. In fact, joy is an integral component of wealth. The joy you feel is both a result of having wealth and a part of the process of manifesting that wealth in your life. What makes you joyful? What motivates you to get up each day and get excited about what you're going to do that day? Where do you think joy fits into wealth?

The Value of a Plan

Sometimes people approach magic as something that will solve all their problems. They fall in love with the fairy tale stories where the Fairy Godmother makes everything alright with a swish of her wand. What they forget is that inevitably the magic goes away and the protagonist has to solve her own problems in order to achieve the fairy tale ending. They also forget that there's always a price for magic.

If you are approaching wealth magic from the perspective that it will solve all your financial problems or just problems in general, you're fooling yourself. That approach to magic is a reactive approach that might temporarily solve a problem, but before long the problem or a similar one rises again. How many times have you heard stories where someone did magic for money, got the money, used it and then was back in a similar situation? Magic didn't solve the problem. It just put it off.

To make wealth magic work for you, you've got to be proactive with it. This means you have to sit down and put together a plan, as well as figure out what actions you need to take. That probably doesn't sound very magical, if anything it sounds very similar to creating a business plan. But the truth is that a plan is a very magical act when you consider that developing it involves defining your results, developing your processes, implementing actions to realize the processes, tracking the effectiveness of your actions, and determining if the result has been realized. That's not different from how I work or most other magicians work with magic. If you don't have a plan, then you don't have a defined path for achieved your desired result. The formation of a plan is similar to forming intent for a magical act. A plan provides you clarity and helps you focus on the desired result, much as intention also focuses you on achieving a specific result.

We'll discuss how to create a plan throughout this book, but for now I want you to look at your definition of wealth and then define the results that will show you that you've achieved that definition of wealth. I'll admit that as of the time of this writing I haven't achieved the results I'm looking for, but I have made considerable progress toward achieving them. My desired results are to be a self-employed, financially independent, debt free business owner who has time to write books and work on projects that genuinely interest me, while also empowering my target clients, either in their business or in their magical practice. I also want to eat a healthy diet, with the right portions, while also maintaining a daily routine of meditation and exercise. Finally I want to have a relationship with my wife where I am fully present and focused when I'm with her, while also being a good role model for my step kids and a good friend to my friends.

At the time of this writing I am self-employed, semi-financially independent, have some debt, but I have time to write books and focus on projects that interest me and I am empowering my target clients in their business. I've launched the Process of Magic correspondence course which is empowering my fellow magicians, and I'm about to launch a space/time correspondence course. I am meditating every day and exercising almost every day, while also changing my diet to eat less and also healthier food. My relationship with my wife, family, and friends is continuing to evolve in a way that is healthy for all involved. I'm working my process and even though I haven't achieved all of my desired results, I'm continuing to make progress by consistently following the plan I've developed. Some of that is due to magical work, and some of it is to due mundane actions that support the magical work (even as the magical work supports the mundane action). My point is this: If you want to be wealthy develop a plan and work towards it EVERY DAY. Make it a proactive part of your life that you are dedicated to, and understand that for it to be successful you must be committed to working your plan. Remember there is no such thing as an overnight success. Anyone who seems to be an overnight success will tell you that there were years of effort that went into achieving that success. What made the success happen is that the person works toward their goals every day.

The Value of Internal Work for Wealth and Money

I mentioned earlier that just thinking your way to wealth doesn't work, but with that said it's very important to do internal work in regards to your values and beliefs about money. The first part of your wealth magic plan involves doing internal work to discover what your values and beliefs about wealth and money are, so that you can make changes if you need to. And I'm going to guess that if you're reading this book, you probably aren't happy with your current level of wealth or your level of money. The true work of the magician begins from within, and then extends outward. The magician needs to work with his/her internal reality and put it in order in order to effectively work with the reality around him/herself. This principle also applies to wealth and money.

We learn our beliefs and values about wealth from our parents. We also learn our money management skills or lack thereof from those same people (Dominguez and Robin 1991, Kiyosaki 2000, Eker 2005). If you are fortunate your parents put a lot of thought into how they model their management of their wealth and explain why it's important to do so to you, but the reality is that most people aren't that fortunate. Most times your parent didn't even know about wealth or think of it as something that will be attained when they retire (as I define it). Instead you learn bad spending habits and living paycheck to paycheck to acquire things you don't need, while putting yourself into more debt. You worry about how to make ends meet without a safety net in place when the next crisis comes. You are merely surviving. All of those activities are just symptoms of dysfunctional behavior that was ingrained in you by your parents, friends, and popular culture.

To change that dysfunctional behavior and the underlying values and beliefs we need to do internal work to discover the core behaviors we have around wealth and money. As I mentioned above, wealth and money aren't necessarily one and the same, but the values and beliefs we have about money can just as easily transition over to wealth. Let me illustrate that with a story.

My Dysfunctional Money and Wealth Values

Neither of my parents really talked with me about money. My dad always seemed to have a lot of it, while my mom was always struggling and worrying about money. She tried to talk with me about money, but what I really got from her was a message of, "You have to struggle in order to be happy." She certainly seemed to struggle, still does to this day, and although I can fairly credit her for teaching me some money management tricks, she mainly imprinted on me the understanding that happiness was hard to come by. Such a dysfunctional belief consequently contributed quite a bit to not only my money issues, but also my wealth issues.

In October of 2006, I started working with the element of Earth and, not surprisingly, my issues with money AND wealth came to the forefront. I read Robert Kiyosaki's *Rich Dad, Poor Dad* and I agreed with the central premise of the book: that dysfunctional beliefs about money could keep a person poor, and that such beliefs were learned from the people who modeled their money habits to us. Reading that book made me realize I didn't want to work for someone else the rest of my life and that I knew next to nothing about how to handle money for the long term. While I could manage the money I had, I was living paycheck to paycheck with no plan for my life.

I was living in Seattle at the time. I hated living in Seattle. The energy of the city just drove me nuts and I didn't like the long commute to work or anything else about the city. I'd visited Portland a couple of times and I loved it. I came alive when I was there. As one acquaintance put it, "Up in Seattle you're really depressed, but when you come to PDX you become so animated and alive." He was right, and my ex-wife and I decided to move to Portland, but then I suddenly developed this desire to stay in Seattle even though I hated it there. Everyone was perplexed, and me more so than anyone because Portland represented wealth to me in terms of the energy of the land, the people, and the culture. So why did I want to stay in Seattle, which represented anything but wealth?

I did some meditation as well as some exercises from *Secrets of the Millionaire Mind* by T. Harv Eker, and what I discovered was that I was holding on to limiting beliefs I'd gotten from my mother: namely that I had to struggle before I could experience happiness. Talk about eye opening! Working through those limiting beliefs cleared up my indecision about leaving Seattle, and in short order I moved to Portland and landed a job that I started within two days of my move. Eker notes the following: "As humans, we are a part of nature, not above it. Consequently when we align with the laws of nature and work on our roots - our 'inner world' - our life flows smoothly. When we don't, life gets rough." (2005, p. 13) Simply put, but there is an element of truth to it. The internal work you do sets up the reality you experience. This isn't to say that only thinking of success will you make successful. You have to marry your thoughts to your actions if you want to change your life or the environment around you. However, it is worth recognizing that how your thoughts contribute to your experiences can teach you an essential truth to magic and life: You are what you think yourself to be. Your thoughts influence and prompt your actions. If you have limiting beliefs and thoughts, they will limit your awareness of the actions you can take. If you have positive thoughts, those thoughts will help you discover more possibilities.

In my case, recognizing that the belief that I had to struggle to have happiness helped me see I was the only one holding me back from moving to Portland. The recognition of those thoughts allowed me to see them for what they were and make changes in my internal beliefs that consequently changed my actions as well. I also realized that I likely had other dysfunctional issues that contributed to my ignorance about money and wealth. Consequently I chose to do a lot of internal work (meditation) on deprogramming limiting values and beliefs that my family had taught me about money and wealth.

Nonetheless, even after the move to Portland, I was still focused on living day to day and still didn't have a plan for my life. Even though the book I mentioned above helped me realize how I was stopping myself from moving away from Seattle and helped me recognize how I was limiting myself with negative thinking, it didn't automatically solve my problems by teaching me how to think positively. It didn't address deeper questions such as "What am I called to do?" or "What is my ideal life and what can I do to create it?" The book told me to think positively, but it didn't offer a plan or even a method for creating a plan. Other books along similar lines didn't offer anything beyond the admonition that I needed to think positive thoughts to create a positive life.

It wasn't until I read *Your Money or Your Life* that I began to ask and answer those deeper questions. The answers helped me realize I was unhappy with my career and that I wasn't following my calling. That book helped me realize I needed to create a plan if I was going to live my life on my terms, instead of continuing to live on other people's terms. I have created a plan and it is manifesting into reality as a result of making it a part of my daily life. This focus on creating and implementing purpose driven actions is what makes people successful.

Part 1 of Your Plan to Create Wealth in Your Life

The first step to developing your plan involves exploring your issues with money and wealth. Until you understand your beliefs and values around money and wealth and consciously choose them as representative of what you truly want out of life, you won't be able to create an effective plan. If, in your discovery of your beliefs and values, you find them to be dysfunctional and limiting, then it will be important that you work to change them, so that you can create your plan toward manifesting your ideal life.

Exercise

I want you to take a moment and think about how you learned to manage your money. Did your parents talk with you about finances or did you learn by observation? What were the lessons you learned? What are the beliefs and values your parents have about money and wealth? Are your beliefs and values similar to theirs, or different? Why are they similar or different? Are you happy with those beliefs or do you feel they limit you?

Answering the above questions can be helpful, but you may also find it useful to meditate on money and wealth. The Taoist water breathing technique is an excellent meditation that can help you discover and unlock areas of tension in your body that are related to limited beliefs and negative emotions. To do the meditation, touch your tongue to the roof of your mouth and breathe in and out through your nose. As you breathe in, draw your internal energy up from your belly to the crown of your head. When you exhale allow that energy to flow into your body, and follow it with your conscious awareness. If you encounter areas of tension in your body, don't try and force your energy through those areas of tension. Instead allow the energy to flow around the tension, gradually dissolving it. Think of the tension as an ice cube, and your energy as water. Eventually the ice cube will melt, as will the tension. When the tension melts, don't be surprised if you feel emotions arise or have memories come to mind. Allow yourself to feel the emotions and experience the memories. What do you feel? What do the memories reveal?

Define the Reward, Your Values, and Beliefs

If you want wealth in your life, the first step is to define the reward. What does wealth look like in your life? What do you want it to look like? How will it feel to actually be wealthy? After you've defined what wealth is, then you need to look at your beliefs and values and determine if they align with that vision. Meditation can be a useful tool for exploring your values and beliefs around wealth (or anything else for that matter), as the exercise above illustrates, but we can also create a vision board that allows us to express those values and beliefs in a visual and textual format.

A vision board can be a textual and visual collage, or it can be pictures. Whatever you put on the vision board needs to embody the theme of your vision. So, for example, if it's wealth you'd pick pictures, phrases and words that represent wealth in your life. I find it useful to use a vision board to define the reward of wealth so that it shows what I am aspiring to. See below for an example of a vision board I created for 2013.

Creating a vision board is easy to do. Make sure you either have a blank bulletin board or a blank piece of paper. If using a bulletin board, you'll need pins, and if using a piece of paper or poster board you'll need glue. You'll also need scissors to cut words and images out of newspapers and magazines and/or a printer, if you want to print something from online.

When I create a vision board I spend the first day cutting the images and words I want to use. I clear my mind when I do this and just look through and cut, without thinking about it too much. Let your intuition guide you to the right images and words that embody your vision. You may not end up using everything you cut, but the point is to simply cut words and images until you feel like you've got all the raw material you need.

On the second day, the glue or pins come out. Start creating your vision board. Glue or pin the words and images together, creating a vision of your desired reality. Make sure you use pictures of activities you want to do, but don't hesitate to include a stack of money as a picture or use phrases that embody wealth in other ways. Remember to include pictures of your loved ones, friends, etc., as well as hobbies and activities you enjoy doing. The activity of creating the vision board is a magical one. You are embodying a desired reality via the vision board.

Once you are done creating the vision board, hang it on your bedroom well or your office. It's something you should look at every day, but it's also something that should eventually become part of the background, influencing your subconscious every day. Your subconscious will soak in this desired reality and start influencing your actions so that you can manifest it into reality. I have done this practice each year, and the vision board for each year has come true because I've been influenced by the vision board each day. Even if I'm not consciously thinking about it, my subconscious is thinking about it, and feeding the desired actions that I need to take into my consciousness so that I can perform those actions. The vision board is the visual embodiment of your definition of wealth and your life (if that's the intention you put into it). Use it to guide you to your desired reality.

I've Defined Wealth, Now What?

Once you've defined your beliefs and values around wealth, you'll start to notice changes in your behavior and actions around wealth. The reason is simple: your actions align with the values and beliefs that you've proactively created. The importance of consciously defining your values and beliefs around wealth is that it allows you to control your relationship with wealth. When your relationship with wealth is no longer dictated by dysfunctional values and beliefs, you have a level of control over your wealth that is amazing because you actually are considering how you will make it work for you. However, it's important to also work proactively on strengthening your new definition of wealth.

An activity which really helped me redefine my values and beliefs about wealth involved reading books on finances and on wealth, but also books on relationships and even different spiritualities. While there are a couple new-agey books on the subject out there, the majority of books available on the topics of finance and wealth are good ones to read. You'll find some books cited in the bibliography that are useful for helping you examine your values and beliefs around wealth. Reading those books opened my eyes to other perspectives and helped me explore what I thought wealth was, not only in terms of money, but also in terms of my romantic relationship, and my friendships, as well as my spiritual beliefs. Now you might find that part of your definition of wealth is reading about technology. If that's the case, then read books on technology as well. Whatever you consider wealth to be, expose yourself to other peoples' perspectives about it. This will enrich your life immeasurably and help you start to discover possibilities that bring more wealth into your life. The question is, what will you actually do with the wealth that you manifest in your life?

Defining What You Will Do with Your Wealth

Part of the internal work that needs to be done around wealth is defining what you will actually do with wealth once it is obtained. As I tell business owners, if your end goal is to make money, then you are operating in a gap. The reason is simple: If you don't know what you'll use that money for, then just having it doesn't amount to much. If you have a plan for how you will use the money, then you have an end goal that recognizes that money is a means to an end as opposed to an end alone.

I approach wealth as an embodiment of my identity. As

such I recognize that I don't "have" wealth so much as I manifest wealth as part of who I am. A successful manifestation of wealth includes how you apply wealth to your life. For example, my embodiment of wealth includes paying down debt while building up savings and managing existing investments on the financial part of my life. On the business part of my life it means building a business, services and products that I believe in, which allow me to help other people improve their lives. On a romantic front, my wife and I have chosen to create a marriage of intention and proactive resolution of issues, while also doing activities that help us enjoy each other and fall in love even more deeply than we already are. As a step-parent, it involves teaching my children how to embody their own version of wealth in a mindful and proactive way. I could add further examples, but the point I'm getting at is that the manifestation of wealth as an embodiment of your life is something best done as an intentional action, which means you need to really get clear on not just what wealth is, but how it will manifest in your life.

Remember my definition of wealth? Wealth is the means to support your lifestyle, while allowing you to pursue your chosen calling. You may not pursue that chosen calling during your day job, but you might use your day job to support your ability to follow that calling. The point of wealth isn't to be a multi-millionaire (though that can be quite nice). The point is that wealth is a means toward helping you achieve a result that embodies what you want all aspects your life to look like. If you focus on what you will use wealth for you will be more motivated to manifesting wealth in your life, as opposed to waiting for it to happen to you.

Exercise

Take a moment to review your definition of wealth. How will you know when wealth is manifesting in your life? What activities will you be doing that indicate you are wealthy? How will it feel to do those activities? What else will indicate that you are wealthy? What else will you apply your wealth to in terms of activities, friends, career, romantic partner, etc.?

Conclusion

By doing internal work on your beliefs about money and wealth you should have a better idea of what you really want, as well as an indication whether or not your internal values support that desire. Additionally, you now have an idea of what you will actually use your wealth for. Once this foundational work has been done, you can turn your focus toward establishing your wealth identity, which will be used to help you embody wealth in your life.

Chapter 2: Creating Your Wealth Identity

Understanding your beliefs and values about wealth is only the first step in mastering wealth. The application of those beliefs and values is what creates your wealth identity. In *Magical Identity*, I explained that your identity is an ontological state of being that describes your relationship/agreement with the universe. Your wealth identity is a facet of your overall identity and it describes how you embody wealth in your life, which can also be explained in terms of how you handle money, and relationships, as well as the overall quality of your life. The proactive wealth magician creates his/her own wealth identity and recognizes that any wealth magic is derived from that wealth identity. If you have a wealth identity where you don't feel wealthy, then it can be useful to create a new wealth identity. Remember that your wealth identity is not about how much money you make, but about how satisfied you are with the quality of your life.

The core of your wealth identity is formed through your values and beliefs, as well as through your attitude. Your attitude is the emotional motivation you feel toward life. The emotions that drive and motivate you will show up in your attitude. If fear motivates you, then fear will always play a role in your decisions. The same is true of the other emotions. Attitude is also represented in the kind of thinking you employ to deal with situations. For example, if you are a negative thinker, you will find ways to prove that a situation is as sucky as you think it is. If you are a positive thinker, you will find possibilities in every situation because you will believe that as long as something is possible, there is a way to make it a reality. Think of attitude as the application of your beliefs and values to the world through your emotions and thoughts.

The creation of a wealth identity is the adoption of a persona that encourages you to find ways to bring wealth in your life. A wealth identity operates on the mindset that wealth is discovered through possibility. As a result, you need to get rid of negative thinking, and words and phrases such as "impossible" or "I can't". In *The Magic of Thinking Big*, David

Schwartz notes, "To do anything, we must first believe it can be done. Believing something can be done sets the mind in motion to find a way to do it" (2007, p. 101). A simple principle, yet one that is very effective, especially when you apply it as a life principle. When you adopt such a mindset your mind focuses on developing solutions instead of dwelling on circumstances. That is the essential attitude the wealth magician needs to cultivate if s/he is serious about manifesting wealth in his/her life.

To adopt that particular principle you need to monitor your thinking. If you find yourself thinking in negatives, stop and ask yourself if thinking in the negative is really helping you. Chances are you'll find it isn't, so reframe your thinking. If you are thinking you can't do something, tell yourself you can do it. If you find that your thinking is leading you to a foregone conclusion, change it around to discover what other possibilities are out there. You might, as you read this, tell yourself that what I'm asking is hard. Change your thinking by telling yourself it can be easy. After all, it can only be as hard or as easy as you make it!

Adopting this principle of positive thinking and believing that something can be done has really opened doors in my life. I used to do a fair amount of negative thinking and it limited me at a few crucial moments in my life. However, ever since I've focused on using positive thinking in every situation, I've been able to catch my negative thoughts and turn them into positive thoughts, and this in turn has allowed me to discover possibilities and solutions where previously I only focused on the problem and how it was limiting me.

Positive thinking of this kind is different from the law of attraction in the sense that you aren't just thinking that you are wealthy and trying to attract wealth to you as a result of those thoughts. Instead you are using positive thinking to help you discover possibilities and take action to realize those possibilities. This principle recognizes that positive thinking is truly effective when it is married to action. Positive thinking without action is really just wishful thinking.

Survive Versus Thrive

I sometimes characterize negative and positive thinking as

survive thinking and thrive thinking. Survive thinking, negative thoughts, is primarily concerned with doing whatever it takes to survive, and is always looking for the negatives in order to plan for them. Survive thinking has its place and use, especially when dealing with a crisis as it can help you assess the crisis and develop actions to get through it. However, people end up spending too much time in survive thinking and this has a detrimental effect on their health and well-being.

Thrive thinking is positive thinking. The sky is the limit with thrive thinking and it represents a positive state of being that focuses on possibilities and expansion. Instead of seeing the negatives, you see the positives in every interaction. Like survive thinking, thrive thinking has its place and use, especially in helping you embrace and explore possibilities for your life. It's not as helpful in situations where there is a crisis, although what it can do is help you "make lemonade out of the lemons".

Exercise

Write down how survive thinking shows up in your life. When you are in survival mode, what are you thinking and how do you experience the world? You may want to even stand up and express it through your posture and movements. How do you hold space when you are in survive thinking?

Next, apply this same exercise to thrive thinking. When you are thriving, what are you thinking and how do you experience the world? Stand up and allow your posture to reflect the thrive thinking. How do you hold space when you are in thrive thinking?

Once you know how you think and how you feel in either mode of thinking, you can learn how to switch either mode on or off by creating an anchor. An anchor is a Neuro-Linguistic Programming technique that is used to activate specific behavior, thinking, and feelings in you. Just by standing up and expressing how you physically hold space with survive and thrive thinking, you've already gotten an experience of what an anchor can be.

Stand up again, and allow yourself to experience survive thinking in how you stand. As you experience this form of thinking and feeling, ask yourself if there is a particular gesture or motion you associate with it. For example if you find that you play with your hair when you are in survive thinking, that would be an example of a motion that you could use to evoke survive thinking when you feel a need for it (It could also help you be aware that you are engaging in survive thinking). To enter that state of thinking you'd simply do the motion or gesture to trigger the anchor. If you want to break the state, you need to come up with a different gesture or motion that you can use to transition from survive thinking to a different form of thinking.

Let's say that you are in survive thinking and you want to go into thrive thinking. What you'll need to do is create an anchor that embodies thrive thinking. So allow yourself to experience thrive thinking again. Is there a gesture or motion that you do that you'd associate with thrive thinking? For example it could be snapping your fingers or whistling a tune. Whatever it is, you'll use that gesture or motion to evoke thrive thinking.

Once you have an anchor for both states of thinking, you can switch back and forth between them at will. Do the gesture that triggers the anchor for survive thinking. Then when you want to, do the gesture that triggers the anchor for thrive thinking and you'll switch from survive to thrive. I recommend creating anchors for both forms of thinking because they can each have their uses. Sometimes you do need to focus on survival and other times on thriving. Recognizing when to call either state forth can be a useful exercise in wealth magic, as you'll know exactly when to use either state to help you deal with situations and discover possibilities.

Focus and Positive Thinking

What makes positive thinking effective is your ability to focus on what you want to manifest into reality. For that matter, focus can make negative thinking equally effective. The best way to observe this is to simply track your thoughts and what you focus on. If you consistently focus on negative thoughts, you will also generate negative results, because you are looking for them. However, focus is more than just that.

Focus is the crystallization of intent, the realization of

desire, and the actions needed to achieve your goals. When you are focused, you are present with what you desire and you are taking action instead of just talking about it. When you focus, you are defining your result and driving your thoughts and actions toward achieving it, and this can work both positively and negatively.

Think about a recent negative result that occurred in your life. What were your expectations around that result? What beliefs and thoughts did you entertain about that result? How did those beliefs and thoughts contribute to the actions taken or not taken by you?

Think about a recent positive result that occurred in your life. What were your expectations around that result? What beliefs and thoughts did you entertain about that result? How did those beliefs and thoughts contribute to the actions taken or not taken by you?

You can use focus as a tool to help you turn your positive thinking into reality. Focusing is a conscious use of directed attention and when you apply it to yourself, you'll find that you'll start taking more conscious actions to achieve the outcome you desire. You use focus to make what you want become an essential part of your existence that must be achieved by whatever means it takes.

Habits

Habits are another way your wealth identity is applied to the world. Habits are activities we do without really thinking about them. A good example is brushing your teeth. You likely don't think about brushing your teeth that often, beyond recognizing that your mouth needs to be cleaned. Brushing your teeth is a habit you've learned to do, and although you may think you do it because your teeth will be clean, there is another reason you do it. You do it because when you brush your teeth you feel a tingly, pleasurable sensation that is derived from the toothpaste. That sensation is the reward you get for brushing your teeth and it's part of what motivates you to clean them (Duhigg 2012).

The anatomy of a habit can be broken into the following components: Cue, Routine, Reward, and Craving. The Cue is the stimulus that prompts the person to do the routine and then obtain the reward for doing the routine. The reward typically also leaves a person wanting more (craving) which is how a habit is sustained. Your habits are also supported by your physiology, specifically the Basal Ganglia. The Basal Ganglia is responsible for automating habits. It ensures that you respond to the cues by doing the habit that you formed in response to the cue. This provides you the reward, both in terms of the actual reward and the neurophysiological response to the reward, which is the release of pleasure neurotransmitters such as endorphins and dopamine (Duhigg 2012, Ellwood 2007, Ellwood 2013)[1].

Understanding the anatomy of your habit and how your physiology supports it can help you consciously recognize how your habits contribute towards your wealth identity. If you find that you are a compulsive spender, than consciously recognizing your spending as a habit will help you explore why you spend money compulsively. Similarly if you recognize that you eat out a lot, but don't feel that you have much money at the end of the month, then you can explore that habit of eating out to discover what it is giving you. All habits give you some kind of reward. Even if a habit is destructive, such as smoking cigarettes, there is a reward that keeps the person doing the habit.

It's very important to recognize that if you want to change your wealth identity such a change will also include changing your habits. You can't change how you relate to wealth without changing some of your habits. The key to changing a habit involves changing the routine that is caused by the cue and continuing to offer a similar reward that fulfills the craving that the cue prompts.

Exercise

I want you to take an inventory of your habits and analyze how they contribute to your current wealth identity. What are your habits? What are the rewards they give you and what are the costs? You might create an excel spreadsheet or table with the following information:

---

[1] See Inner Alchemy and Magical Identity for more detailed explorations and explanations of neurochemistry.

Habit	Reward	Cost
Smoking	Feel distressed, feel good when I smoke.	I cough a lot. The cost of a pack of cigarettes is $5.95 per pack and I buy 3 packs a week.
Eating out	I don't have to make food or clean dishes	I have to pay a tip and eating out costs more than buying ingredients. Some of the food is unhealthy.
Reading and discussing a book with my partner	We can discuss the book together and share what we think about it.	Price of the book (unless we borrow it from the library).

As you can tell, I have chosen a couple of examples that could be considered "unhealthy" and one example that could be considered "healthy." Whether these examples are or aren't healthy depends on how you evaluate and define them. For the purposes of this exercise, I want you to catalog all of your habits. What you'll likely find is that most of them have a monetary cost and all of them have a time cost.

Cataloging your habits is useful for understanding your daily behaviors and determining how they contribute to or take away from your overall sense of wealth. Look through your list and evaluate each habit. Is it a habit you want to continue, or do you want to change it? How will changing it contribute to your sense of wealth?

If you want to change a habit, you need to change the routine and still provide yourself a similar reward. The cue will stay the same, since it is a stimulus that prompts the habit, but you can replace the routine with something different. For example, if you feel bored, instead of watching T.V., go for a walk. The reward will be similar in the sense that you are exposing yourself to new visual sights, but you'll have an additional reward in terms of how your body feels as a result going for a walk.

Changing the routine may not be enough. Because habits are automated by the part of the brain called the Basal Ganglia, you can find yourself sliding back into old habits. I've found that working with your neurochemistry can be useful for stubborn habits. I've covered in detail how you can do this work in *Inner Alchemy*, and *Magical Identity*, but I'll briefly cover it here.

You will want to work with your neurotransmitters as spiritual entities. You'll want to work with GABA and Glutamate (neurotransmitters essential for forming or changing habits), and likely Dopamine and Endorphins (the pleasure neurotransmitters). I recommend doing an initial meditation where you contact each neurotransmitter and get a sigil from them that represents their spiritual essence. You'll use the sigil to call them and work with them directly. After you've connected with the neurotransmitter entities, do a meditation where you travel into your brain, specifically the Basal Ganglia. You can use the neurotransmitters to change the neural pathways in your brain that support the habit you want to change by redirecting which synapses and receptors are activated when the stimulus (cue) for the habit occurs. Refer to the books I mentioned for more in-depth exploration of this technique.

You can also proactively create habits. Although habits become automated behavior, when you initially learn a habit you have to consciously focus on it. Thus when you first learn to ride a bike, it takes a lot of conscious attention to pull it off. However, once you've learned how to ride a bike, the Basal Ganglia and muscle memory kicks in and automates your ability to ride the bike. Let me share with you an intentional habit I've created that keeps me focused on my work.

The White Board Habit

Because I am a business owner, I've had to create specific habits to keep me on task with my projects. I work at home a lot of the time and it can be very easy to get distracted by household chores, television, Playstation 3, or any other number of distractions waiting in the wings. So I've chosen to create specific habits that help me stay productive and allow me to reward myself with a distraction once I've gotten a set amount of work done.

My cue is a white board, and more specifically the list of projects I need to work on (such as writing this book). I only put important projects on the whiteboard. Activities I'd do every day, such as update my social media status, are left off the board. I know I'll do those activities as part of my daily marketing work. The important projects typically involve either client work or work on a writing, video, or other creative project that I'm doing as a way to create products for my businesses. My goal, on any given day, is to wipe at least two items off my white board or make significant progress toward getting rid of those items. The white board is never clear of projects. Once I finish one project, another one goes up on the board.

I have my white board set up near the door to my office. If I am feeling bored or restless, when I swing my chair around the white board is the first thing I see, and it reminds me of the projects I need to work on. It's a cue that focuses me on the routine of getting the work done. If I get two or three items wiped off the board or make significant progress on them (which is noted on the board), than I give myself a reward. Typically the reward is a half-hour to hour long walk or an hour of Tae-Bo exercising. I've chosen taking a walk or exercising as a reward because it keeps me in shape, feels great, and helps me clear my mind. Not surprisingly, when I get back from a walk I usually work another hour or two and then give myself the evening off (usually when my wife comes home from her job).

As you can see, this is an intentional, proactive habit. I've designed it to keep me focused on my work so that I can get specific tasks done and make progress toward growing my business. I've designed a specific reward as well that reinforces my desire to stay on task and get things done.

You can apply what I've done here to your own habits in your workplace or your business, or any other part of your life. Pick the cue first. What is it that you will use to stimulate the need to do your routine? Then pick out your routine. What activity do you need to do to meet the need expressed in the cue? Finally pick your reward. What will you give yourself as a reward for doing the routine? The creation of these intentional habits will allow you to create wealth positive behavior that helps you generate more wealth in your life.

Set Points and your Wealth Identity

Your wealth identity is also defined by a concept called Set Points. In *Financial Sorcery*, Jason Miller defines Set Points as control systems that dictate a number of factors in a person's life including, wealth, health, love, and even spirituality (2012). When you try to diet or change your approach to money, you are influenced by these Set Points. Think of them as gravitational fields that determine the degree of effective change you can accomplish. Unless you move your Set Point, you can only change so much. For example, if you are dieting you might accomplish a temporary change, but once you are off the diet you'll probably find yourself back at the same weight you were at before. In order to make a permanent change, you need to move your Set Point. The creation of intentional habits, as well as the internal work you've done with your beliefs and values about wealth can help you move your Set Point. However, you may also find it useful to apply more overt forms of magic to moving your Set Point.

In August of 2012 I did a ritual to help me change my wealth Set Point. I felt back then that I was hitting a wall when it came to the amount of money I was bringing in, as well as feeling doubts about my business (something that happens to every business owner), so I decided that I'd do a Set Point movement ritual to move my wealth Set Point.

Throughout 2012 I'd been working with the spirit of the Dragon. I was born in the year of the Dragon, and since 2012 is the year of the Dragon once again, I thought I'd capitalize on that connection. The dragon is considered a being of power and wealth, and I felt he'd be perfect work with for this ritual. I decided that I would invoke Dragon, allow him to possess me, and in the process literally move me and my wealth Set Point. To do the invocation I settled on using body paints. I painted my body in patterns that represented my connection to Dragon. Once I was finished painting my body, I invoked Dragon.

When Dragon entered into my body, he took over the physical movement. My body slithered and walked like a dragon would, and while this was occurring, the dragon expressed my wealth point through movement. When I slithered on the ground I was at a low Set Point for wealth, but gradually

Dragon moved my body upward and in the process moved the wealth Set Point as well. After the actual movement was done, Dragon and I entered into a shared trance state where he proceeded to instruct me on how to permanently change the Set Point. I followed his instructions, which included reading *The Magic of Thinking Big* and changing my prices and frequency of consultation. In a month's time I landed two new clients who were happy to agree to my rates and my frequency of service. I also completed two virtual courses. Since that time I've continued to work on changing my Set Point by reading books and taking classes on various business topics while implementing what I've learned into my wealth practices. That ritual set up the necessary momentum to push me past the wall I came up against, and since that time the momentum has been maintained with this and other Wealth Magic workings.

If you want to apply some pop culture magic to your Set Point work, you could choose to do a magical working where you work with a pop culture persona that embodies wealth. You could do an invocation or evocation of the pop culture persona, depending on what you want to accomplish. Invoke if you want to learn specific behaviors or attributes. Evoke if you want the entity to actually help you in specific ventures you are working on. Make sure you do some research on the pop culture persona you want to work with, as there are plenty of celebrities that may seem wealthy, but are actually dealing with debt problems of their own. For example, you might consider working with the pop culture persona of Warren Buffet, Bill Gates, or Steve Jobs. What attributes do you want to draw on? What attributes do you want to avoid drawing on? You can model your behavior off of a famous person or a pop culture persona, but be sure to draw on the behaviors that are most beneficial to you. For example, if I were to work with the persona of Steve Jobs, I'd likely not want to draw on some of the more negative aspects of his behavior. I'd focus on drawing on his creativity and innovation, and his ability to visualize the future of technology and business. I'd filter out the rest of his personality because I wouldn't want to deal with his negative behaviors. If I were to evoke Steve Jobs, I'd likely evoke him for help with working on a specific technology venture.

Your Wealth Identity and Other People

Jason recommends, and I agree, that you also surround yourself with people that embody the level of wealth you want to manifest in your life. When I first started working with wealth magic in 2006, I noticed almost immediately that the majority of people I associated with had poor attitudes toward money and wealth. As I worked on changed my beliefs and values about wealth, I found myself becoming more distant from those people, and also attracting people into my life that embodied the wealth Set Point that I wanted to reach. Since then I've focused on developing relationships with people that embody a specific attitude and approach to wealth that I want to cultivate in myself.

The people you surround yourself will either support your wealth identity or try and tear it down. You will quickly be able to tell by how they respond to the changes you make in your life. For example, when I began seriously exploring finances I was told that spending so much time on money made me less spiritual. I realized the person who made that comment felt threatened by my choices and was trying to discourage me and keep me at her level of wealth identity. Consequently I chose to disassociate with her because I knew that she was trying to sabotage me. This isn't to say that you should stop your friendships with people who have different wealth identities than your own, but rather you need to recognize that some people will feel threatened by your choices to make changes to your wealth. Additionally you will find that who you choose to spend time with does impact what those people can offer to you in terms of advice or suggestions. Jason notes, "The simple truth is that if you want to get rich, you should try to develop friendships with people who actually are rich...If you tell your rich friends that you are buying a rental property, they will ask you about whether you are using the right tax loophole, what property manager you are using, and other things to make sure you do not lose your shirt" (Miller 2012, p. 98). The point is that people who have a similar wealth identity or one that is wealthier than yours will have a different level of information and advice than someone with a lower wealth identity.

We choose people in our lives because we identify with

them and what they embody in their lives. Choosing to be very conscious about the people we want in our lives is a good activity to perform because it teaches you about what you really value and what you really want to manifest in your life. It also teaches you to recognize people who might be dysfunctional or saboteurs in your life. Cultivate your relationships carefully and remember that those you want in your life are people who believe in you and support you. Remember that you also need to be willing to support and believe in them. Good relationships are never one way.

One of the skills involved in cultivating relationships is networking. Many people think of networking as people meeting and exchanging business cards, but genuine networking is about forming relationships with other people by getting to know their needs and problems. A good networker is someone who is always looking for ways to help other people, specifically by connecting them to other people. Networking doesn't always involve attending business meeting. You could belong to a hobby group or go to a "meet up" and you could still be networking. Networking can also involve participating in activities that you'd associate with specific subcultures. For example, if you wanted to learn more about the kink community you might go to a munch, which is a networking event for kinksters. As pagans and occultists we have a number of "networking" events as well, such as Pagan Pride Day. A networking event is an event where you go to connect with a given community and learn more about the people involved in that community.

Wealth Identity and Appearance

Although it may seem superficial, clothing is another way you can explore your wealth identity. A person's appearance can influence how other people treat the person. Appearance isn't just clothing, but clothing is a major part of how people evaluate other people. A person's appearance affects how people treat that person, and even whether they will hire that person. Appearance can also include makeup, jewelry, tattoos, and how you smell. All of these aspects of appearance have an impact and your awareness of them can be useful in a variety of ways. I also think of appearance as metaphysical, in the sense that the energy and attitude you put out can make a big difference. If you have a negative attitude, people will be repelled by you. If you have a positive attitude, they will be attracted to you.

For example, if you want to offend someone one of the easiest ways to do it is through appearance. Because people are so quick to judge, you can use appearance as a weapon. Likewise, if you want to attract or impress someone appearance can help you make the right impression. I think of appearance as a glamour that is comprised of your attitude and emotions, your body language, the clothes you wear, and the overall image you want to project to the world.

With wealth magic, it can be useful to cultivate specific types of appearances for specific situations. For example, when I go to my Chamber of Commerce meeting or a networking meeting, I dress in a business suit, and the image I project is one of a professional who is also empathetic and understanding of the needs and problems of others. Since my daytime profession is that of a Business Coach, it's important for me to cultivate that particular appearance in those situations. Conversely, at pagan festivals or meet-ups I dress in more colorful and less business oriented clothes. Nonetheless I even consider those clothes to be part of a professional appearance, albeit as an occult author instead of a business coach. I know that if I dressed up in my business coach attire for a pagan meeting I would be related to differently than when I wear clothes that are more appropriate to the pagan setting. Similarly, if I wore more colorful occult author clothes to a chamber meeting, at the least I'd get some weird looks. When I am at neither type of event, I dress casually because I'm not dressing to fit into either group of people.

The choice to change your appearance to fit in and interact with a specific social group shouldn't be thought of as superficial. If anything it is a magical act, a change in identity used to help a person gain entry into a specific group of people s/he wants to associate with. While appearance alone doesn't guarantee acceptance, it can go a long way toward helping you open doors and meet people that will help you gain access to that social group.

Exercise: Clothing Glamour/Invocation

Think of your appearance as a glamour or invocation. The assumption of your appearance is your choice to assume a persona of your wealth identity that is used to embody the wealth you want to manifest in your life. Each piece of clothing you put on is part of a ritual designed to make you embody your wealth identity. When you put the clothes on you deliberately call up the energy, the attitude, and the belief that you are whatever wealth identity it is you want to manifest. Feel the identity wrap itself around you with each clothing article you put on. What will you look like? How will you act? Who will you interact with? How will all of this help you manifest your wealth identity?

Your appearance is a form of magic because it is used to embody the kind of social groups you want to interact with. If you want to interact with people who have a different standard of wealth, and you want to learn from them, invest in your appearance. Go out and buy a couple business suits from Goodwill where they are cheap but still very serviceable. Then go to a business meeting and observe how people treat you. Do they act differently because of how you are dressed? Chances are they do simply because appearance is indicative of your desire to get to know them and meet them on their terms. Remember as well that wealth isn't just about how money you want to make. You may not want to join a local business organization or network and that's fine. Your definition of wealth needs to factor in the type of people you want to spend time with. Just remember that if part of your definition of wealth differs from the majority opinion, you may find yourself making changes to your definition of wealth in order to fit in.

If your definition of wealth involves being part of the in-crowd in the local goth or hippie community, than plan on buying attire that will help you connect with those people. Again, while appearance alone won't guarantee acceptance, it will open the door. At that point it's up to you to start talking to people and getting to know them and what interests them. Your appearance is part of your life and business plan, so put some thought into how you want to appear and how that will help you manifest your wealth identity.

Conclusion

Your Wealth identity is comprised of your values, beliefs, and attitudes about wealth, and it is expressed through your habits, appearance, and the people you associate with. The rest of this book will show you how to create a proactive wealth identity, but examining your wealth identity as it is now is important for understanding where you are and recognizing what you want to change.

Supplemental Resources

Visit magicalexperiments.com/wealthmagic and download my free habit assessment tool.

Chapter 3: Money Management, Debt, and Magic

When I think about money, I don't think of a credit card, dollar bill, or coin (all of which are physical expressions of money). I think of money as this primal, elemental force that has been with us for as long as recorded civilization. I think of money as an elemental force because of how it moves people and what it can move them to. Money can move a person to beg, steal, and even kill someone, or it can move someone to give, work hard, and slave away their lives for some kind of security that is illusively promised.

I differentiated money from Wealth, and the reason is simple: having a lot of money doesn't automatically make you wealthy. If anything, the prime emotion behind money is fear, and the primary desired result is security. When you look at typical fears people have around money, the fear is: "Do I have enough money to make ends meet each month?" This is typically known as living from paycheck to paycheck. Add in fears about having enough for retirement and/or paying off debt, and the result is money ruling you. This is why so many people work at jobs they hate. They are serving money and using whatever money they get to try and ease their own misery. Dave Lee notes:

> Wealth is abundance where and when you want it. To elaborate, to be wealthy is to live your life the way you want to. The condition of wealth is the experience of confidence, relevance and abundant pleasure in one's material environment. Money is a parameter, whose value is arbitrary and impersonal; Wealth is a skill, whose value is arbitrary, and personal. Money is a spirit, an elemental; Wealth is the attribute of a God. (2011, p. 14)

Wise words. Money isn't Wealth. Wealth is an attitude, a way of life, while money is a tool. The problem that faces people the world over is that they mistake having money as denoting Wealth, and having lots of money as having lots of wealth. On the other hand, using money as a tool to become wealthy is helpful. I haven't met any person who doesn't have a lot of money that can prove s/he is wealthy. Money is a tool that allows us to live life the way we want to if we properly use money as a tool. Many, many people could be wealthy if they learned to use money as a tool, instead of enslaving themselves to acquire it and its results (consumerism). People work for money instead of making their money work for them. Personally I prefer the latter option.

If money is an elemental force (as I posit that it is), then we need to understand that elemental force and consider how we can apply it to our lives in the most beneficial ways possible. We've already recognized that fear and security inform the emotional composition of the elemental force of money, but another aspect of money that is useful to recognize is that money loves to move. The rise and fall of the stock market, credit card debt and interest, interest on savings, dividends, etc., are all indicators of the movement of money and the fact that money prefers to move. What's really interesting to consider is that money's movement is usually not in favor of the individual, but instead favors corporate entities. For example if you consider that your savings account typically has a measly interest rate of 1% and compare that to the interest rate you get on a car loan (3.5% in my case), you'll note that the interest is weighed in favor of the bank or loan institution. That's not counting the high interest rates typically associated with credit cards. You can do better via the stock market (if you know how to play), but even then you're still dealing with the reality that the reason you have good returns is because of the company and how money is framed to support businesses over people. The fact that you benefit has more to do with the fact that you've directed your own monetary resources toward supporting companies that will hopefully produce a return that improves the flow of money for investors.

So money moves, but how it moves tends to support businesses, which in turn support the movement of money. It shouldn't be surprising that as an elemental force money is looking out for itself. It will naturally support the institutions that support it and cause it to thrive, and if that happens to be detrimental to you, that's no real concern to money. The question is...how can you make money work for you, instead of you working for it?

Another aspect of the elemental nature of money is consumerism. Part of how money supports businesses is by motivating people to spend (i.e. move) it on possessions. You know the feeling well. You've just gotten paid and the money is burning a hole in your pocket. You keep aside enough for the basics, bills and groceries, and the rest is spent on some item you want or eating out, or on cigarettes. Whatever your fix is, that's where your money goes. Money wants to be moved, and consumerism of any kind is another way for it to keep moving.

The one thing money doesn't want is to stand still. Keeping it in your checking account or under your bed doesn't allow it to move. It just stagnates. Money doesn't want to stagnate. It needs to move in order for it to really thrive. Money wants to move and it wants to move you as well. Whether it moves you to spend money or invest it doesn't really matter. All that matters is that movement is generated, because movement is what keeps money alive.

I asked the question above about how you make money work for you, and the answer is that you recognize it wants to move and you make it move in the direction that benefits you. By making money move in your favor, you can make that elemental force generate wealth for you. However to do that, you need to be familiar with how money is moving you. I've described that above, but let's apply it to your life.

What are Your Money Habits?

Money habits are habits based on money, specifically what you do when you have money. Think of money habits as the behaviors that demonstrate how money moves you. If you put part of your paycheck into your savings or invest it, that's a money habit. If you spend your money on eating out and buying the latest tech toys, those are also money habits. In order to effectively understand your money habits, you need to list them. If you are keeping track of your expenses on a monthly basis this will be easy, but if you aren't, you will need to start doing so. You can visit magicalexperiments.com/wealthmagic for a free financial form if you need one for your financial tracking.

Tracking your habits involves tracking specific behaviors. So what you need to do is create a spreadsheet or chart that shows how much money you bring in each month, and then shows where that money goes. Take a look at the example below:

	Jan	Feb	March	April
Paycheck	3,500	3,500	3,500	3,500
Transfer to savings	100	100	100	100
Groceries	453	506	489	535
Eat out	85.87	25.36	63.51	14.06

As you can see this example shows how much money you are bringing in, what is going toward savings, as well as what is going toward groceries and eating out each month. You'd ideally track this activity for each month. You'll also want to include other categories such as car payments and insurance, rent/mortgage, credit cards, but also expenditures such as cigarettes, video games/hobbies, and pet expenses. Every time you spend money, keep the receipt and input it into your tracking sheet.

By doing this activity, you will be able to understand where your money is flowing and what your money habits are. I recommend updating your spreadsheet every day or every other day, so that it only takes a few minutes. If you wait to do it once a month you may end up losing receipts or get lazy about keeping an accurate record. You want an accurate record of your expenses so that you can decide if your money habits are helping or hurting you and your wealth identity.

Once you have a record of your money habits, take a look at them. What do your habits look like from month to month? How do you feel about those habits? Are they contributing to your wealth identity in a positive or negative way? Whatever your answer is, don't guilt yourself over your choices. The point of this exercise is that it helps you understand your relationship with wealth and with money from a holistic perspective. Until you track how you spend your money, i.e. how it moves you, you can't really know how effectively you are utilizing it. Once you do have that record you can start making changes in your money habits. For example, when I first did this exercise, I realized I was spending way too much on eating out, and it not only impacted my wallet, but also my health. By examining my money habits, I was able to change my eating out habits, which not only helped me save money, but also helped me lose a bit of weight and eat healthier.

If you are a self-employed business owner you want to also create a spreadsheet for your business. You might already use Quicken or Quickbooks to generate profit and loss reports for your business, which is useful information to have, but I find that having a business spreadsheet provides me a way to track my monthly profits and expenses in one place. I do use Quickbooks, but I use my business spreadsheet to complement my financial records on Quickbooks and provide me that holistic perspective on where the money in my business is moving.

Money Management and You

Once you know your money habits, it's time to focus on money management. Many people are good at short term money management, where you pay your bills on time, buy your groceries and have a little left aside for fun stuff. However they may not be good at long-term money management, which involves cultivating an emergency savings, IRA's and stock investments. And that's not even addressing debt, such as credit card debt, auto debt, student loans, etc.

Go back to your money habits spreadsheet. On another page, set up the following table:

Taylor Ellwood

Assets	Total (Jan)	Total (Feb)	Total (March)	Total (April)
Roth IRA	16,000	16,000	20,000	20,000
Emergency Savings	9,000	10,000	11,000	12,000
Debts				
Credit Card	545.98	1,600	1000	238
Auto payment	232.17	232.17	232.17	232.17

You should add any assets you have including mutual funds, cds, stocks, annuities and anything else you invest money into. If you aren't doing any investing you want to start, because your investments operate on the principle of making your money work for you, and even making other people's money work for you (we'll discuss this in more depth later).

You want to also include all of the debts you have, as well as how much you are paying each month. Each credit card should have its own row, as should any student loans you have, car payments you make, mortgage, etc. You will have debt of some sort, but ideally you'll have as little as possible. If you have a lot of debt, your first priority will be able to get rid of it as soon as possible. After that you want to develop an investment plan that allows you to make money no matter what time of the day it is. Remember that money likes movement. As such your approach to money needs to always be informed by this magical principle so that you can capitalize on it.

Once you know what your total debts and assets are you can begin planning your financial goals as well as the magical work you'll do to help you reach those goals. The best place to start is with your debt.

Debt Management

Take a look at the spreadsheet that lists your debt payments. I'm going to have you create another spreadsheet now, which will display the following information:

Type of Debt	Current Debt	Credit Limit	Interest Rate	Total Debt
Credit Card	8,323.23	12,000.00	10.9%	
Credit Card	6,932.13	14,000.00	12.9%	
Car loan	20,231.45	N/A	3.5%	
Mortgage	236,232.00	N/A	4%	271718.81

The purpose of this spreadsheet is to help you track how much debt you have, as well as how quickly you are paying it down. You want to put every kind of debt you have in it so that you have an accurate record of how much money you owe, what the interest rates are, and an overall total. It may feel overwhelming to have a snapshot of your total debt, but having such a snapshot will help you develop a strategy for paying it off.

Any approach to debt needs to factor in what your total is, as well as the interest rates so that you can determine where to focus your efforts to pay off your debt. Typical wisdom suggests that you start with the lowest amount of debt first, so to use our example above, you'd pay the bare minimum on all of the debts except the $6932.12 debt. With that one you would add whatever money you could to the minimum payment to help pay it off quicker. Once you paid that debt off, you'd then pay off the next largest debt, and so on and so forth.

However you may also find that you don't want to just focus on paying off debt. It is a good idea to have no credit card debt, but after the credit card debt is finished, you might find that you also want to focus on investing money for your retirement. While it is good to pay off your car and house debt, it's also important to recognize that a sound financial strategy plans for the future as well as dealing with the present. I recommend paying all your credit card debt off and then putting a small monthly payment on each credit card you have, so that you can pay it off each month and keep your credit score high. Once you've paid the credit card debt off, you can still choose to put more money toward your car or house debt, but put at least some into stock investments, IRAs and other forms of investments that provide dividends.

Regardless of how you approach debt, it's important that you develop a strategy that allows you to pay the debt off while also capitalizing on the principle of money's desire to move. My own approach to debt has always factored this principle in.

Asset Management

I cover assets in more detail in the next chapter, but for the purposes of keeping you on with the financial tracking tool, I want you to create another spreadsheet with the following information:

Type of Asset	Current Investment	Interest Rate	Total Assets
Roth IRA	55,000	2.5	
Rental Property	800/month	0	
Stock (NIKE)	160,000	4	
Stock (Intel)	350,000	4	
			565,800

I've simplified the example a bit, but for all intents and purposes this spreadsheet would be used to help you track assets and determine how much you have available for retirement and other needs. You could also add emergency savings to this list as well as any other type of asset such as a money market account, CD, 401k, etc. The key thing is to keep this spreadsheet updated so that you have an accurate record of what you have in terms of assets. This will help you make smart financial moves. I'll go into assets in more depth in the next chapter, but let's return for now to debt and how to manage it.

Money Moves: My Debt Reduction Strategy

In August of 2008, I had no credit card debt, and $10,000 in emergency savings. My ex-wife (who I was still married to then) was getting ready to go back to school, and it even looked like we might be able to start investing our money. I had started my coaching practice part time, and worked as a tech writer full time. I didn't like the job I was in and I decided to quit after I was entirely blamed for a problem that was only partially my fault. I quit the job, and started looking for work. I had a good interview and things looked promising. Then the economy crashed in September 2008 and all my job prospects dried up. I decided to go into business full time, but, as I was to discover, the first year of owning a business takes a lot of work and sees little profit, especially in a depressed economy.

Fast forward to 2010. My ex-wife divorced me and I was left with two credit cards that had significant debt and a business that was only bringing in a bit of income, and even that income wasn't steady. Fortunately, Kat came into my life shortly after, and although she also brought some credit card debt with her, she also brought the capacity to hold down a steady job, as well as her fervent belief in my success as a small business owner. In 2011, we made a couple financial mistakes, such as signing up for a timeshare service, but after those mistakes were made, we pulled out my copy of *Your Money or Your Life* and started following the program. We also realized that we needed to get on the same page about our financial values if we were going to pay off our debt and start saving for retirement. We also wanted her kids to have better financial skills than the ones they were learning from their father.

In the fall of 2011, Kat and I had 5 credit cards, with debt on each card. It seemed almost impossible for us to pay it off, but we focused on paying off the smallest debts. We also figured out the interest rate for each card and evaluated which cards needed to be closed down. And I employed the principle of money moving to our advantage, because I also looked at how we could transfer credit debt from one account to another. We ended up getting rid of two credit card debts by simply transferring the debt over to another card. Money wants to move, and we accommodated it, but we did so in our favor. We then focused on paying off the smallest credit card debt. By 2012 we were down to two credit card debts, with both balances steadily getting smaller.

I also had car payment that was fairly expensive and had a steep interest rate. I decided to look into switching the car payment over to a different financial institution, and it turned out I could do so, and get a cheaper interest rate. By doing some research I discovered how to take the principle of money movement and turn it into an advantage for us by consolidating debts, while getting lower interest rates for those debts. This allowed us to lower our debts and number of payments, as well as the interest being charged. Most recently we consolidated all of our credit card debt into one monthly payment and put all of our cards away, with the understanding that we wouldn't use them until the debt is fully paid off. While at the time of this writing we are still paying off our debts, we are much closer to paying them off than we were in a year before, and we've paid over half the debt we owe on the credit cards. All it took was a willingness to capitalize on the concept that money loves to move and explore how we could get it to move in our favor.

Behavior, Habits, and Debt Reduction

Capitalizing on the principle of money movement is a good start to getting your debts in order, but it's also important to recognize the correlation between your debt and your spending habits. If you are a person who feels compelled to keep up with the Jones, or to buy the latest Apple technology, you may find that you have expensive habits that keep you piled in debt. While moving money around can help you manage some of that debt, you also need to manage your spending habits. Otherwise they will manage you and you could end up with a lot more debt.

For example, if you smoke cigarettes you know it can become an expensive habit. A pack a day can cost over $5 per pack, which adds up quick. You can bum cigarettes off other people, but eventually they'll get annoyed and start withholding. Add in health issues, and the resultant costs associated with those issues, and smoking becomes an expensive habit. People who have quit smoking tell me how surprised they are at how much more money they have and how much healthier they feel, simply because they aren't smoking anymore.

However, you might have a different habit. For example you could collect comics. Your average comic book now costs around $4. If you subscribe to 10 comics, you are paying $40 a month to collect those comics. How often will you read them? Or do you think they'll have a lot of value down the line and plan on holding on to them in the hopes that you'll sell them someday? You don't want to stop reading comics, but that $40 could go toward actual bills or household needs. I suggest getting creative. You can actually get graphic novels at your library which have the collected issues. Then you can read the comics without paying a cent. You can apply this as well to books, renting the majority of them from your library without incurring any costs. Undoubtedly you have rationalized why you need to buy the book or comic book, but you only have so much time and space for such things. While a house full of books looks nice, those books are a pain to move and take up a lot of space, plus you can only read so many books at a given time. While it is nice to own a comic book or book, you also have to evaluate the Return on Investment (ROI). How many times will you read said comic or book? How much space will it take up? How much will time will it take for you to earn that comic or book? That last question is the most important question you can ask.

You exchange time for money when you work at a job or own a business. Actually what you really exchange is your life for money. While you can get interest on money, you can't get time back. Once it is spent, experienced, etc., it's gone, so it is very important to be certain that you are spending your time in the most efficient manner possible. If you are going to spend money, you should spend it on something that will give you the maximum return on investment for the time involved working for it. This is why credit cards aren't a good way to pay for something. While they allow you to buy something, if you don't pay it off that month you are hit with interest, which means that the return on time shrinks because you have to work that much more to pay for what you bought with the card. Ideally you only buy something if you can actually pay for it upfront or pay it off within the month. For example, I paid $500 cash for the computer I'm typing on. If I paid for it with a credit card and didn't pay the card off immediately, I'd also be paying interest for each month the $500 remained on the card. That means that I not only have to put time in to earn the $500, but also the interest that is added to the $500. The time spent on earning the interest is time that is wasted, because your return on investment is diminished.

I only buy something if I know that I will get more time out of it than the time it takes me to earn it. For example, I buy video games at $60 per game, but I know I will easily get at least 80 hours out of a game. I am still playing games that I bought in the 1990's because I enjoy them and enjoy the opportunity to play them again. The return on investment I get with my games is worth the money I spend for them, because I know I'll easily make up the time spent earning the games by playing the games.

What you buy defines you and your habits. You want to invest money in habits that are healthy for you. One of the biggest problems with cigarettes, alcohol, and drugs is the fact that they are habits of consumption. Once you smoke a cigarette, it's done. You've smoked away the money AND time you spent to earn the cigarette and the return is minimal. You get a nicotine high for a little bit, and then you're back at square one craving the sensation. You spend more money and puff more of it away for a fleeting sense of satisfaction that nonetheless leaves you unhappier because you want more. The result isn't worth the cost of the habit, either monetarily or emotionally. Your habits can put you into debt, especially if they are habits that involve consumption of substances that create addictions.

Take a look at the spreadsheet you've created to track your monthly spending. Any expenditure that isn't for bills or groceries are expenditures that you are putting toward habits. Whether your habits are healthy or unhealthy, if they put you into debt they are costing you in time and money. I want you to re-evaluate those habits and see what you can stop spending money on, even if it's only until you get your debt paid off. For example, one of the habits I stopped spending money on was comic books. While I enjoyed reading them, I realized they were contributing to my debt. Instead of buying comics, I now rent them from my library at no cost. The benefit is that I have more money I can put toward my debts, and I can still enjoy the comics I like to read.

You can apply this thinking to other habits as well. Instead of buying your morning latte at Starbucks, why not brew some coffee at home? Instead of getting lunch at the office cafeteria, why not brown bag your lunch? Making little changes in your spending habits can make a big impact on your budget and free up money that you can put toward your debts. Not only will you pay your existing debt off faster, but you'll also cut down on the debt you are bringing into your life.

Some habits that cost you money may be hard to change. If you are a smoker or you like looking at pornography, you'll find it harder to change those habits because they are addictive habits. The physiology of your neurochemistry supports addictive habits. However there are ways to change your habits, provided you are willing to work on both the behavior and neurochemical levels of the habit.

On the behavior level, a habit is comprised of a cue, routine, and reward (Duhigg 2012). The cue is the stimulus that prompts the habit. The routine is the actions of the habit. The reward is the feelings you get when you have done the habit. If you want to change a habit, you need to replace the routine with a different one that provides a similar or better reward than the one you are currently getting. You also need to consciously monitor the cue, so that when it occurs you don't fall back into doing the old habit, but instead consciously choose the new habit.

On the physiological level you are dealing with neurotransmitters such as dopamine and endorphins as well as the Basal Ganglia, which automate your habitual behavior (Duhigg 2012, Robinson 2009). Dopamine and endorphins are reward neurotransmitters that make you feel good when you do an action that stimulates the receptors in your brain. For example when you smoke a cigarette or have an orgasm, dopamine and endorphins will be triggered to "reward" you for doing those activities. This neurochemical reward can cause addiction because it causes the brain and body to crave more of the sensations that it experienced.

A Magical Exercise for Changing Your Habits

This exercise is comprised of two levels of magical work. One level focuses on behavioral changes to your habit, and the other level focuses on the physiological changes needed. I recommend integrating both levels into your work to change a habit, as a two-pronged approach is more effective at reinforcing the desired behavior and reward over reverting to a bad habit.

On the behavior level, identify the habit that you want to

change. Specifically you'll identify the routine you want to change. For example, if you don't want to smoke any longer, you need to replace the routine of smoking with a behavior that will still supply a similar reward. With smoking the neurochemical reward is a stimulation of endorphins, which cause you to feel pleasure, so any activity you do needs to provide a similar reward. Exercise is an activity you could that would not only replace smoking, but help you get healthier and provide the feeling of endorphins while also helping you work through any frustrations you feel with quitting smoking.

To reinforce this new habit, you can also use the NLP technique of anchoring, which allows you to embody and activate a specific state of consciousness by using a gesture, word, or action to invoke that state of consciousness. If you want to change your smoking behavior one of the challenges you face is figuring out how to support that change, especially if you can't do the replacement habit every time you feel the urge to smoke. While chewing Nicorette could help, why not also explore creating an anchor that you can use each time you feel the urge to smoke and can't follow through on that urge? For example, you could take a gesture you associate with smoking, such as putting two fingers to your mouth and deeply inhaling to invoke a state of consciousness that you associate with pleasure. To create an anchor do the following steps:

1. Feel and/or visualize the ideal state of awareness you want to feel. If it is a state of happiness or pleasure, than focus on feeling that happiness and pleasure. Visualize memories that brought you a state of happiness and allow yourself to fully feel the happiness. Give yourself a couple moments to feel it, and then shake yourself out of it.

2. Next pick out the gesture. In this case, we'll pick a gesture with smoking. Take two fingers and put them to your lips. Keep the fingers slightly parted, as if you were holding a cigarette. Now take a deep breath in through your mouth and after you've inhaled, let you hand move away and exhale. That gesture will be the anchor for the state of happiness you've just felt. The reason you'll use the gesture is because you want to change your smoking habit. The best way to change a habit is to take any

gestures you'd associate with that habit and rewire them to the new habit.

3. Do the gesture again, but this time when you inhale, feel the breath also bring in the embodied state of happiness. This action allows you to anchor that state of happiness to the gesture, so that every time you do the gesture it creates that state of happiness.

Anchoring is useful because it allows you to embody a state of being that counteracts stress or other feelings that might prompt you to go back to the old habit. When you get the urge to do an old habit, you can use your anchor to short circuit the urge, while also providing you with a state of being that empowers you to stay on track and focus on your new habit. You can apply anchoring toward any habit, not just smoking.

On the physiological or neurochemical level, it can be useful to work with your neurotransmitters as spiritual entities. Your brain is a wonderful tool that can automate a lot of your behavior. This is good when you are learning how to ride a bike, but not so good when you want to change a bad habit. While modifying your behavior can help you with changing a habit, it can also be useful to work on the physiological level.

To work on the physiological level you need to identify what neurotransmitters you will work with. Using the smoking example, it would be important to work with the neurotransmitter Endorphin. However you also want to work other neurotransmitters as well. GABA, glutamate and peptides are other neurotransmitters that will be useful to work with for changing habits (as I'll explain in more depth below). In order to work with these neurotransmitters you need to treat them as spiritual entities. I will provide a brief explanation here on how you can work with them, but I'd also suggest reading *Inner Alchemy* and *Magical Identity*, where I go into much more detail.

To work with a neurotransmitter entity, you first need to contact it. This involves putting yourself into a meditative trance state and using that state to move your consciousness into your body and more specifically your brain. Once your consciousness is in your brain you want to call to the neurotransmitter asking it to appear before you in whatever shape it wishes to appear as.

Once it appears, ask it for a symbol that you can use to call it for any work you do with it in the future. You also want to ask about what it does and how it can help you. Afterwards you may want to do some research and discover how accurate the entity described itself. From my own experience, I've had received accurate descriptions, but it's always important to verify the information the neurotransmitter entity provides you,

In our example above, you would need to make contact with endorphin, GABA, glutamate and peptides before you could begin the work you wanted to do. Once you contacted them and understand what they can do, you could do an advanced working where you would reroute synaptic pathways from your old habit to a new habit. The working would involve using GABA to shut down the old neurochemical pathway and neuron that supports the habit you want to change. You would also use Glutamate and Peptides to redirect endorphins to a new neuron, which would be used to support the new habit you are creating. To automate this process, I'd recommend coming up with a sigil that allowed you to call on the powers of the respective neurotransmitters. Thus when you felt the urge to smoke, you'd visualize this sigil and use it to re-route your neural pathways from the old habit to the new habit. The sigil would activate the appropriate neurotransmitters to make sure the re-routing was occurring.

How does all of this relate to Wealth Magic? If you can change your habits, then you can also change the costs involved in sustaining those habits, which means you can free up money to help you pay off your debt. One of the reasons people stay in debt is because they don't look at what they can change in their environment or themselves that will help them free some money up and make it easier to pay off their debts more quickly. Yes, changing some of your habits means sacrificing some comforts, but it can also make paying your debt off much easier than it would otherwise be. And remember that we're not just saving money right now by changing a habit, but also down the line. While not all of your habits are unhealthy, the ones that are unhealthy will provide you more debt in terms of medical help and other issues that arise as you get older. Look at your spending habits and ask yourself which ones are really necessary. Then make some changes. You don't even need to stop buying every single thing you like, but choosing to change a couple habits can have an impact on your money.

What About Money Spells?

I'm not a big fan of spells or doing magic to get money into your life. Typically, if you are doing magic to get money to come into your life, you're likely doing it as a reaction to a problem that you think money will solve. And while getting money to appear via magic could solve that problem, what will you do the next time another problem occurs? At some point doing magic to get money will either fail or have you dealing with a circumstance of tragedy you'd likely prefer to do without. Additionally I think that people resort to money magic because they don't want to think about money. They figure that if they get the money they need, they'll never need to think about it again. The problem is that you can never get enough money when you have that mindset. Something will come up that requires you spend it and you'll be back to thinking about it.

A proactive approach to money accepts that you need to think about it, and more importantly you need to develop a proactive awareness of it and how to work with it. The spreadsheets I want you to create are a tool you can use to get a handle on your relationship with money and start planning on how to get it to move in your favor instead of against you. Developing a better relationship with money and learning how to manage what you bring in will help you handle the occasional problem or crisis much better than doing a spell to get money at the last minute. Wouldn't you rather just do without the stress and have a focused approach to handling money that lets you go to bed knowing you can handle an emergency without having to sweat over the details?

I did a money magic spell once. Actually it was magic to help me get a car, but it boiled down to being a money magic spell. I needed a car, and I couldn't afford to buy one and didn't have much of a monthly income (being a graduate student at the time). I needed the car because I was starting to do a lot of talks on the pagan festival circuit and I knew if I wanted to reach some of those festivals I would need to provide my own transportation. I also felt that having a car would make my life a bit easier in terms of getting groceries or being able to visit friends. The public transportation I had access to was rather limited. I wanted to buy a car without having to deal with monthly payments, and I knew I needed to make sure the insurance was affordable and would still do more than cover the bare minimum.

My "spell" was the comic book Sigil technique that I've written about in *Space/Time Magic*. I drew three squares or panels and in each panel I placed a sigil that represented a desire I wanted to manifest into my life. One sigil was for the car, one was a troublesome co-worker, and the last one was for a school situation. I drew lines between each panel and colored the lines and sigils. Then I did some sex magic to charge them and burned them to fire the sigils. The underlying principle involved was that instead of charging and firing one sigil, I'd charge and fire three sigils, but I'd first connect them to each other so that whichever sigil manifested into reality first, it would pull the other two desired possibilities into reality as well.

It worked. Within a few days my dad called me and told me that he wanted to help me buy a car (I hadn't said anything to him prior to doing the working). He felt that I needed a car and he knew I wouldn't be able to afford one on my limited stipend. He told me to look for one, and when I found it to let him know and he'd send me the money. I found a car, he sent money, and I had a car to drive within a couple weeks of doing the working. So my money magic worked, but notice that it relied on a relative providing me money. That was the most likely possible source of money I would have access to. The limitation of doing money magic is that while it can work, it's not going to win you the lottery. It will draw on the resources you have access to which could involve a family member or friend, or your work. In the latter case, it could help you get a raise, but as we'll explore in a later chapter on job magic, it's better to have a proactive approach to getting a raise as opposed to getting one just so you can handle a problem.

In the case of this example of money magic, I did think about why I needed the car and how it would improve the quality of my life, as well as my ability to reach far flung pagan festivals. There was some consideration of the long-term benefits of having the car, and so the working wasn't entirely based on a reactive approach to handling a problem, but the problem with the working was what resources I had to draw on. I didn't have a lot of money so I needed to draw on a resource that did have money. While nothing happened to my dad, other than him suddenly choosing to help me with my car situation, I realize in retrospect that there could've been worse consequences. I didn't plan for any of those consequences possibly occurring. Doing magic to get money can work, but it takes effort, there can be consequences and it would be so much easier if you just get proactive about your relationship with money and learn how to manage it effectively so that you can handle problems that come your way.

Recently I did another comic book sigil working. This time I was much more careful about the details and thought long and hard about how I could make the working be a proactive wealth magic working as opposed to a reactive wealth magic working. I'd actually been invited to participate in a sigil game on a Facebook group, and part of what I considered was how I could make the wealth magic working applicable to the people who were going to be charging the sigils.

I decided that I that the comic book sigil working would focus on generating wealth in my life in five different ways: First, it would bring into my life resources and education that would help me improve my areas of weakness in my business: marketing and sales. Second, it would help me determine what wealth magic I could best use to help me enhance my marketing and sales. Third it would provide me opportunities to get in front of prospects. Fourth it would help me get this book published by the publisher of my choice. Fifth and finally it would help me cut out any financial spending that was detrimental to my household and business. And for the people who were charging the sigils, it would help them discover the aspects of their identities that they most needed to work on in order to improve their lives.

I did this working in December of 2012 and January of 2013. The people who charged the comic book sigils reported changes in their lives shortly after doing the working that were consistent with helping them work on aspects of their identity that they needed to address. As for myself, I ended up getting access to several classes and resources for free (when ordinarily they'd cost a lot of money) that have helped me improve my sales and marketing. I did determine what wealth magic to do to enhance my skills (which I share later in the book), and I started getting more speaking opportunities, which has also led to more business. I've also changed some financial spending habits and at the time of this writing, this book is in consideration by the publisher I wanted to publish it.

By putting some thought into this working, I am generating long last changes that will improve my business and life, with no potential detriment to anyone in my life. That is the best way to approach wealth magic. Be proactive, instead of reactive.

Conclusion

After having read through this chapter (and hopefully done the exercises) how do you feel about money and its place in your life? In the next chapter we'll explore how you can invest money for your retirement. Your relationship with money isn't the entirety of wealth, but it is the foundation on which your wealth rests.

Supplemental Resources

Please visit magicalexperiments.com/wealthmagic to get free financial tracking tools.

Chapter 4: Money Management, Investments, and Magic

In the previous chapter we discussed how to manage your money and reduce your debt. However, getting out of debt isn't enough. While having no debt is a good thing, you also need to plan for retirement and other situations that arise. Knowing what to do with your money is an essential part of wealth magic, and this especially applies to planning for your future.

Emergency Savings

Emergency savings is a financial tool that is a must for every family. If you don't have an emergency savings account, stop reading and go to your bank or credit union and get one started NOW! Even if you are in debt, you should have an emergency savings account. While it is important pay your debt off, you also want to have enough money set aside to handle a crisis without having to go to your credit cards. $1000 as emergency savings is sufficient if you are in debt. Keep it in your savings, and only use it if you have an emergency, such as a car repair. Don't touch it otherwise, for anything unless it's an emergency.

In most financial books I read, its opined that a person should have six months of living expenses saved up in their emergency savings, if they aren't in any debt. I agree with that idea, with the one caveat that if you have a family it changes what six months of living expenses is. Six months of living expenses for two people looks different from six months of expenses for four people. You need to plan your emergency savings accordingly, factoring in the basic needs of your family which includes rent/mortgage, utilities, phone and internet bills, as well as groceries. If you are still paying your car off, factor that payment in as well as insurance payments. The best way to determine how much money you should have in your emergency savings is to tally up your bills for one month and then multiply by 6. That number will provide you a goal for what your emergency savings should look like. Initially, after you've paid your debts off, you should focus on putting most of your available money into the emergency savings so you have it in case you go through a period of unemployment or for an emergency. Its money you will use to help you get through a rough period or to pay an unexpected bill without having to go to your credit cards. If you take money from the emergency savings, it should be replaced as soon as possible to keep it at the six-month minimum.

The interest rate on a savings account is typically around 1%, so while its useful as an emergency reserve, it shouldn't be used as a retirement strategy. Your money won't move very fast in a savings account.

Planning your Financial Future

Once your emergency savings is established, you should start making some plans for your retirement. Even if you are self-employed as I am, there may come a day when you want to retire, and it's important to have a financial plan in place that allows you to do so without having to sweat the details. Some people may feel reluctant to do this step because it involves making investments, but investing doesn't have to be hard and there are resources that can help you make good investments. When you plan your investments you want to keep two principles in mind. One is the money loves movement principle discussed in the previous chapter. The other principle is based on you, specifically how comfortable you feel about taking risks with your investments.

When you invest money, there is always a degree of risk as you are investing your money into a company and hoping that the company will perform well enough to provide a dividend, while also risking the chance that the company won't do as well as you'd like. However if you do some research and get some help, you can make informed investments that bring you a return on investment. Additionally, there are different types of investment opportunities available, but before getting into that, look into some resources that can help you do the necessary research to make an informed choice about your investments.

The first resource is financial books and websites.

Fool.com, which is the website for the Motley Fool, is an excellent resource to draw upon in terms of articles and helpful advice from people on the site. In addition, I recommend *The Motley Fool's Guide to Investments* which covers the pros and cons of different types of investment with great depth. There are additional books you can read on investment, but if nothing else, read that book.

You also may want to talk with a financial adviser. A financial adviser can provide you information and advice about investments and even help you invest your money. The one drawback to a financial adviser is that s/he is going to think of his/her own interests, as s/he is usually paid through your investments. In other words, the investments that s/he recommends are ones that will help him/her get paid. However I have found that financial advisers are quite helpful and can make the process of investment much less daunting than it would be otherwise.

Ameritrade.com is another resource that allows you to make your own investments without relying on a financial adviser. They'll charge you a fee to make sell or buy stock, but that's the only fee you pay.

There are other financial resources available. The bibliography of this book has some other financial books that I've drawn on, and you can always do your own research as well. What's important is that you make the time to do the research before investing your money. Further down in this chapter you'll find some suggested tips that can help you do some of that research.

Types of investments

There are different types of investments you can make. It would be beyond the scope of this book to cover these types of investments in depth or suggest what you should or shouldn't invest in, but I can provide a brief description. I suggest doing more research on your own to learn more about these types of investments and to determine what a good fit is for you.

Mutual Funds - These are funds that are invested in a variety of companies. They are low risk and fairly stable, but the return on investment is also low because you own minute shares of the companies. Mutual funds over diversify, which can be good in terms of safety, but not so good in terms of the return on investment (Gardner & Gardner 2001).

Index Funds - Index funds are a portfolio of specific businesses picked for a fund. For example, the S & P 500 index Fund is comprised of 500 businesses that are used to evaluate the health of the economy in terms of their performance. Investment in these kinds of fund is stable with little risk and little research needed, with a decent return on investment. (Gardner & Gardner 2001).

Stocks - Stocks are investments in individual companies. They can be high risk, depending on the company, but the reward can also be high. You definitely want to research the companies you are going to invest in, and it's a good idea to invest in what interest you (as that should give you an indicator about the performance of a given company). (Gardner & Gardner 2001).

401K - If you work at a company, the company may offer you a retirement plan where if you invest in their retirement plan they will match up to a certain amount of your investment, with money from themselves. There have been some changes to 401k's recently so do your research AND don't plan your entire retirement off of a 401k. While it can be useful for helping you put money into a retirement account it shouldn't be your only strategy.

Annuity - Annuities are paid to insurance companies, which will invest the annuity and then provide payments, when the person reaches retirement age. Annuities are used to accumulate funds that are free of capital gains and income taxes.

IRAs - There are a few types of IRAs: Traditional, Roth and SEP. A Traditional IRA allows you to make tax deductible contributions. Any earnings that are accumulated have no tax impact, but withdrawals from the account are taxed. A Roth IRA allows you to make contributions as after-tax assets, which means taxes have already been taken from the money that is contributed. A SEP IRA is a Self-Employed IRA that allows a business owner to contribute up to 25% of his/her income to the IRA. It's similar to a traditional IRA, but it can allow a business owner to put a lot more money into the IRA, as opposed to a traditional or Roth IRA. All IRA's allow you to make contributions up to a specific amount within a given year. It's ideal to include an IRA in your retirement planning, but don't make it the only part of your retirement plan.

The information I've provided above gives you an idea of how you can invest your money, but I suggest doing more comprehensive research so that you can make informed decisions about investing for your retirement. It is important to make regular contributions to your retirement accounts. Additionally if you have children, you may also want to consider creating an investment account for their education. Check with a financial adviser, who can tell you what your options are for your children. If nothing else, you should try and set up some kind of trust fund specifically set up to help them with education after high school. However, be careful with what type of trust fund you set up. For example, if your kid decides to not attend college and the trust fund specifically stipulates that it can only be accessed if s/he goes to college, you've just lost that money. This actually happened to my father in law. He set up an account for my sister in law, but she chose not to go to college and they lost the money. If he'd set the trust fund up in a less restrictive account she could have had access to it for other things.

Always remember to do your own research. I know I've mentioned it a few times now, but I can't emphasize enough just how important it is to do your research and make sure you know what you are getting into financially. Always verify what a financial planner tells you by either checking in with a second one or doing some digging for information on your own. Remember that you are the ultimate authority of your financial future, which means you need to do the footwork to make sure your investments are actually helping you reach your financial goals.

The Money Move Principle and Investments

The money move principle I mentioned in the previous chapter also applies to investments, especially when you need to make a move on your investments. You don't want to trade your investments all the time, as the fees associated with trades can add up, but you also want to know when to roll investment accounts into other types of investment accounts, as well as when to sell or buy stock. I'm going to provide an example of how I applied the money moves principles to my investments, but I'd suggest that you do your own research before making changes to your investments.

When I quit working for corporations I had a 401k account. I didn't really know what to do with it, but I did know that since I no longer worked for the company, it wasn't getting any money from the company or from my paychecks. A financial adviser I knew talked me into rolling it over into an annuity. I didn't know any better at the time, so I went ahead and rolled it over into the annuity, which actually wasn't a good move because the annuity didn't have a lot of growth. Later, after I'd done some research on my own and met another financial adviser I thoroughly vetted, I learned I could take a specific amount of income from the annuity and transfer it over to an IRA account without any taxes or penalties being assessed to the account. I started making yearly withdrawals and now have an annuity, which has some growth, and an IRA account which has better growth. Both investment accounts are fairly stable, but what is most helpful is that my money isn't completely stuck in a low dividend earning account. I was able to, with some help, make the money move from one account to another, where I could earn a higher dividend.

With investments you need to remember that there is always some level of risk involved. Lower risk creates lower dividends, but also less chance that your money will be lost due to market conditions. Higher risk promises higher rewards, but also higher losses. Your comfort level with risk will determine what investments you make, and you also want to factor in your age when making investments. When you are younger, it is easier to take higher risks and lose some of the money you invest, but when you are older, stick with lower risk investments because you will likely be drawing on that money in the near future.

Money Altars and Magic

I haven't written much about money magic, because in order to effectively do money magic I think you need to have a solid grounding in financial principles. However, you use can magic to interact with money. For example, you can connect with the elemental aspect of money to aid you in your financial decisions. One of the ways you can do this involves creating a money altar. Your money altar is an altar to money and its movement in your life. It should be an altar that you keep in your home office or the room you do your finances in. Your money altar may be one of several altars that are focused toward wealth. We'll explore the other types of altars in later chapters.

My money altar is set on top of a filing cabinet that contains financial records for my businesses, as well as my investment records. I feel that the altar performs two functions. It puts a protective force around my investments and businesses, and it also enhances the movement of my businesses and investments in a favorable direction that will bring in more income and allow me to use it wisely for the prosperity of myself and my family.

My money altar has the following items on it. It has a red Dragon statue, with the dragon clutching a pearl. I've always associated dragons with material wealth and the Dragon is one of the business entities I work with. The pearl is pointed toward my desk. I also have a blue stone, with a gold dragon etched on it, also pointed toward my desk. There is a wedding picture of my wife and I, as well as a calculator and the checkbooks for the personal and business accounts. There is a copy of Manifesting Prosperity, the wealth magic anthology I edited a few years ago, and there is an armored truck with a green sigil painted on it that holds four tubes of different coins.

The money altar is designed to charge all interactions with money with the intent to produce a favorable outcome for family and myself. Sometimes I will place a dollar bill, credit card, or an investment prospectus on the money altar to charge the item with energy from the money altar. I also pray at the money altar each day before I start my work, as a way of offering homage to Dragon and the elemental spirit of money. Any checks I receive from clients are also put on the altar before they are deposited so that they can charge the altar with the inflow of cash, and so that they in turn are charged so that good financial decisions are made.

When I want to work with money as an elemental spirit, I work with it through Dragon. The Eastern dragons, in particular, are known for being mutable in appearance and nature, and I feel that reflects an understanding of money and how money changes. You don't need to work with Dragon to work with money, but I've found it useful to work with some type of wealth entity because that entity has a long, ongoing relationship with money and knows the nature of it very well. The wealth entity can mediate money and its desire to move in a direction that is favorable for you. Naturally, if you choose to take this approach to working with money, you also need to think of what you'll offer to the wealth entity. In my case, I do a weekly offering to Dragon and a monthly full invocation as well. I've also offered part of my skin to him, which has resulted in two dragon tattoos.

Another consideration to keep in mind when working with a wealth entity or with money is that you need to be very specific about what you want accomplished. If you aren't, problems can occur that put you into a situation of less wealth. For example, if you own a side business and work a full time job, you might be inclined to ask a wealth entity for help with your business. However if you don't include very specific information, what you may discover is that the entity's idea of helping your business involves you leaving or losing your full time job so you can work on your business full time. If that isn't what you want, then you need to be very specific about what you want it to accomplish for you, and the same applies to working with money as an elemental force. Always consider the environmental impact (i.e. how the magic will affect your family, life circumstances, etc.) before doing a magical working. This applies doubly so to wealth magic.

Money Sigils

A more direct way you can work with money as an elemental force involves putting sigils on money. I see dollar bills with writing or odd symbols marked on them and I figure the person doing the writing on the bills is trying to communicate with someone or something (Note it is illegal to deface currency. That said, I've yet to see anyone bust someone for it). For that matter, you could also do the same with a credit card or a check.

Your sigil is a symbol that represents a specific desire or result you want to manifest. The classic method of creating a sigil involves writing a statement of what you desire to manifest and then getting rid of repeating letters and using the remaining letters to create a symbol that represents the desire. Another method is called automatic drawing and involves drawing the sigil without trying to control where the pen or pencil goes. There are other methods as well, which can be found in a variety of books on the topic.

Regardless of what method you use, once you have your sigil you can mark it on your credit card or dollar bill. If you are going to put it on a credit card, I recommend the sigil be utilized for a long-term financial goal such as buying and maintaining a house. With a dollar bill, it can be a long or short-term goal. If you use a sigil on a check, I recommend using it to influence the outcome of the situation the check is being written for. When you put the sigil on the dollar, check, or credit card, you want to visualize the specific outcome, and merge it into the sigil. This charges the sigil. You fire the sigil and activate it when you spend the dollar or use the credit card for a purchase. The purchase pushes the sigil into the world and starts the cycle that will manifest it into reality.

Another variation on this method involves coins. You arrange the coins into the shape of the sigil on your money altar, and leave them to be charged by the altar. Then when you are ready to fire the sigil, you take the coins and spend them.

You can also use more classic symbols with your money. For example, if you want to work with the planetary energy of Jupiter, which is associated with Wealth among other things, you could put Jupiter's astrological symbol on the money and invoke that energy into your wealth workings.

Money sigils are useful as a way of activating the power of money for help with specific financial situations. I used the above example of buying and maintaining a house because it's a good example of how to use money magic proactively. A house is an investment of money and time. You'll be living a house for a significant period of time and you'll deal with a variety of expenditures including the mortgage, property taxes, insurance, and maintenance. Such an investment calls for long-term money magic that is used to help you meet the costs of the house, while also keeping you financially sound.

Conclusion

Money magic is just one part of wealth magic, and as I mentioned above educating yourself about finances is the best choice you can make, as it'll help you make informed decisions. However there is much more to wealth magic than just getting rid of debt, handling investments or using money magic to improve your circumstances. In the next chapter we'll explore wealth entities you can work with as well as how to work with them, and then we'll focus on jobs and self-employment.

There is one final note I want to make in regards to money magic. Effective magic is based in part on how much a person understands about the given area of his/her life that s/he wants to change. Effective wealth magic involves developing a comprehensive understanding of wealth as it applies to your life, which also means that you need to be willing to engage the concept of wealth, as well as related concepts such as money. The reason I've devoted a significant chunk of this book to practical aspects of finance and money is because I want you to effectively work with your finances and money, instead of trying to avoid those aspects. Too often people don't want to think about money or finances. Thus they do money magic, play the lottery or do something else in the hope that they can get enough money that they don't have to think about it anymore. The ironic reality is that they end up thinking about money and finances more, albeit from a place of scarcity.

The best way to come to peace with finances and money is to learn how finances and money work, and then learn how you can work with them positively. When you learn to work with money and finances and develop proactive strategies for managing your resources, you'll find that your financial fears diminish and you'll feel empowered. That is the best money magic a person can do, in my opinion. Indeed, when you have a good relationship with your finances, you'll find that the need to do magic for money significantly diminishes, and instead you'll focus on developing proactive financial strategies that will help you maintain and grow your financial wealth while helping you sustain the lifestyle you truly want to live.

Chapter Five: Wealth Magic Deities and Entities

In later chapters I'll be discussing a variety of methods you can use to integrate deities and entities into your wealth magical workings, but with this chapter we will focus on learning about the wealth deities you can work with, as well as how to create wealth entities. There is a difference between a deity and an entity. A deity is a god or spirit that many people know about, and who may or may not be worshipped by said people. An entity, on the other hand, is a spiritual being you've created to perform a specific task. Both types of spirits have their uses and specific strengths, as we'll explore further below.

I'm going to provide a list of possible wealth deities you can work with. The list isn't exhaustive and you can likely find other wealth deities that I haven't covered in this chapter. Whether you choose to work with one of the ones I write about or one you've discovered via your independent research, remember that it is important to treat them with respect. I'm not a believer that a deity is automatically a higher being then any of us, or that it should be worshipped, but I do think it's important to recognize that a deity is a different kind of being than what we usually encounter and that it's important to treat a deity with respect when working with it.

There's also one other item of interest I want to mention about wealth magic deities. Some, but not all, of those deities also have a connection with death and the Underworld. This is only significant in the sense that material wealth comes from the Earth, but is almost a transitive experience and state of being that also returns to the Earth. Inevitably all of us will die and return to the Earth, and however wealthy we were won't be significant at that point, but rather will also return to its own source.

Zeus/Jupiter: In hermetic planetary magic the planet Jupiter is considered the planet of wealth. Likewise Zeus/Jupiter can be thought of as a wealth deity because he is the king of the gods, able to do as he pleases with little consequence occurring to him (though others aren't so lucky). You can work with Jupiter to increase your riches and wealth, or to help you with situations involving justice.

Hermes/Mercury: Mercury is a god of information and networking, but also a god of commerce, especially for business owners. You work with Mercury to get information or help you network, or bring some business through your doors and you might also work with him on investments.

Aphrodite/Venus: A goddess of love can teach you a lot about wealth as well, especially as it applies to relationships. People are attracted to similar people with similar levels of financial acuity and wealth. Venus can help you with networking and relationships, but also in finding people who have the level of wealth you want to embody in your own life.

Hades/Pluto: Pluto is a god of the underworld, but also a god of wealth. He rules over everything that is underground including all the minerals and other valuable resources that a person might want access to. You could work with him in investment magic or to uncover resources that you need access to.

If you wanted to you could also draw on other Greek and Roman gods for wealth related matters. For example, you could work with Ares/Mars or Athena/Minerva in situations involving competition or business strategy. Or you could work with Poseidon/Neptune to teach you how to be more flexible, but also to discover hidden possibilities. The key is to think about wealth from a variety of angles. Which deity fits the angle you need to work on? And the Greek/Roman gods and/ or planets they represent aren't the only wealth deity resources we can draw on...

Ganesha: The Broken tusk Elephant god who removes obstacles and likes to gamble can be a useful wealth deity to work with if you want to take a risk or if you need to remove obstacles and blockages from your life.

Lakshmi: The Hindu goddess of wealth. She is depicted as having golden coins coming from one of her hands. If working with her, she likes it if you spend some of the wealth she provides. Thus she'll gift you with wealth, but expects that you'll be generous in your tipping.

Bune: Goetic Daimon of wealth and death. He provides sound business advice and can also help you with networking. He'll help you uncover business opportunities and provide you strategic suggestions for how to resolve those matters in your favor.

Berith: Goetic Daimon of wealth, specifically as it applies to gaining political offices or exercising political power.

Bethor: An Olympic spirit who can be helpful with job hunting and promotions at work.

Riprinay: A wealth spirit that foresees economic changes. He can help you foresee market changes and also make suggestions on investments.

Euronymous: A Daimon of wealth and death. He operates in similar manner to how Bune operates, but he can also be helpful for helping you discover resources.

Mammon: An Aramaic god of wealth and commerce. You could work with him in business related matters, or to help you with a financial deal you are trying to put together. He is an excellent resource to draw on when looking over contracts.

Dragon: Not a deity per se, but dragons, both Eastern and Western, are associated with Wealth. They can teach you how to save money (being good hoarders of treasure), but also offer some protective resources for wealth magic, as well as show you how to be aware of the movement of money.

This isn't a comprehensive list of wealth deities, and you may know of some I haven't mentioned here, but if you've never worked with a wealth deity before, this will give you a place to start. I suggest doing more research into these various deities if you want to work with them. You can find a fair amount of information online, as well in books, a few of which are in the bibliography of this book. Additionally if you are working within a specific tradition you can choose to work with the wealth deity of that tradition. There is usually at least one deity devoted to wealth in most spiritual traditions.

However the real research begins when you work with one of them. You will need to determine if you have a genuine connection with the deity and if you are comfortable with what it wants in return for its aid. Your initial invocation or evocation will be an interview of sorts, where both you and the deity determine whether or not you can work together as well as what you will provide to each other. If you want something from the deity, you also need to be prepared to offer something in return. It's also important to be aware of the culture and history associated with the deity, because it could affect how you work with the deity or what it expects to get from you.

If you do to choose to work with a wealth deity, it's important to have a dedicated space for the entity, which includes an altar. You'll want to make offerings to the deity you work with. The offerings could be incense that they like, or a candle of a particular color that you burn to honor the deity, or a food/beverage offering of some kind that they desire. I like to make offerings of publicity, where I write about my work with the deity as a way to honor it and show why other people should want to work with the deity. I also create paintings and collages as offerings to the deities. You can make offerings of money to the deity, which could entail making a donation in the deity's name to a charity, or using the money to buy a statue of the deity or some other devotional material. Whatever kind of offering is agreed upon, you need to follow through on it. If you follow through, your wealth deity will follow through for you by providing the services you've agreed on.

For example, the offering I've made to Bune, in exchange for his aid, has been a publicity offer. I have a painting of his seal in my office, created when we first agreed to work together. Every so often I write a post about him on my blog and I'm writing about him in this book. You'll also find his seal on the cover art for this book. Those offerings satisfy him, and in return he offers business advice and help with developing the business plan to grow my businesses. He wants publicity offers because he wants more magicians to work with him, and also because the attention and belief feed him. I'm happy to provide him what he wants, and in return I've gotten help with my business endeavors, which has allowed me to transition out of a business I no longer wanted to do and into a new business, while starting another business on the side.

Working with a wealth deity doesn't mean the deity will do the work for you. While a given wealth deity can help you, there is also an expectation that you will also do the work needed to help yourself. While Bune has given me advice and suggestions, I've always had to choose whether to act on that advice or not. I think that such an approach is best because it insures that you take responsibility for your wealth. Yes, the deity will help you, but it won't take care of your life for you. However, you don't need to limit yourself to working with deities. There are other options that can be just as helpful when it comes to getting aid with the manifestation of wealth in your life.

Wealth Entities: How to Create and Work with Them

Sometimes a wealth deity isn't the right kind of spiritual being to work with or can't offer a specific skill set you are looking for. When this occurs you have two options: you can create an entity with the specific skill set you need, or you can work with a corporate/pop culture wealth entity. For this section we'll cover how to create a wealth entity[2].

The first detail that needs to be addressed is the type of wealth entity you'll create. You could create general prosperity/wealth entity, but it might not address the specific circumstances that you need to resolve. Below are a few types of wealth entities you could create, dependent on your particular wealth needs.

Networking Entity: This is an entity that helps you become a better networker, while also identifying people that you want to

---

[2] See my co-written book Creating Magical Entities for a detailed exploration of how to create and work with a variety of entities.

connect with. It can also act as an opportunity entity in terms of discovering possible people who could best help you reach your goals. This is an ideal entity to work with if you are job hunting, trying to get a promotion, or if you are self-employed.

Opportunities Entity: This is an entity that alerts you to opportunities by giving you intuitive pings about situations, events, and people that you might want to look into. It's not the same as a networking entity because some of the opportunities it alerts you to may have nothing to do with other people, but instead involve discovering the right information or getting access to a particular item that is rare and hard to find. This is an ideal entity to work with in general, but can also be customized for specific types of opportunities.

Job Hunting Entity: This is an entity that helps you hunt for a job. It uses all of your job hunting activities to increase the probability that you will find a job. It can also be helpful in negotiating pay and benefits. This is an ideal entity for job hunters and can be evolved into a job entity that alerts you to opportunities for advancement.

Finance/Money Entity: This is an entity that helps you be more mindful of your finances and how you spend money. It will help you budget your money, offer suggestions on investments, and keep you focused on paying off your debts. It's useful for anyone who wants to improve their relationship with money.

Sales Entity: This is an entity that will help you enhance your sales. It provides intuitive pings about potential clients as well as providing insights into how approach a given sale. It can also provide you information about how to improve your sales technique. This is an ideal entity for anyone in a sales position or a self-employed person who does a lot of sales.

Marketing Entity: This is an entity that helps you become a better marketer of your business. It will help you find marketing opportunities, while also pushing you to be communicate better about what you do the benefits are of working with you. This is an ideal entity for a self-employed person or someone in marketing.

Job Entity: A job entity differs from a job hunting entity because it is an entity that is comprised of your job. It will help you do your job better, get you to stand out to the right people and help you get promotions. It's useful for anyone who is an employee and wants to excel at their job.

Business Entity: A Business entity is the entity of a self-employed person's business. It can provide insights on how to run your business more effectively, as well as indicate when it's time for the business to evolve. This entity is useful for anyone who is self-employed and wants to interact with their business on a more conscious level.

Relationship Entity: This is an entity that helps you with your relationships (romantic or friendships). It can help you be a better lover/friend or it can offer advice/intuitive suggestions on how to deal with a problem in one of your relationships. It can also help you with work-life balance. This is a good entity to create if you want to work more consciously on your relationships with others.

Health Entity: This is an entity that helps you work on your health. It will help you with diet and exercise for your mental health, while also providing a counter balance to negative messages you might tell yourself. It can also help you with work-life balance. This is a good entity to create if you want to improve your relationship with your body and life.

As you can see there a variety of wealth entities you can create. You may find that you need to create multiple entities, depending on what areas of wealth you want to improve in your life. You can create as many entities as needed, but remember that these entities aren't going to take over the living of your life or doing your job. They can help you, but you still have to do the work.

How to Create an Entity

In Creating Magical Entities, there is a worksheet that can be used to create an entity. Below I've included most of the details of that worksheet so that you can create your own entity. The first detail that needs to be determined is what goal or purpose is the entity supposed to fulfill. In other words, you are creating the entity to achieve a very specific purpose or fulfill a specific function within your life. For example, many years ago I created an opportunity entity. Its purpose/function was to find opportunities for me that would be useful for advancing my professional goals.

The next detail that needs to be filled out is a detailed explanation of what the desired results are. What will the result look/feel like? You might also include what you consider to be acceptable consequences for achieving results, i.e. how will achieving the result impact your life, profession, relationships etc. With the opportunity entity, my desired results were that it would notify me of professional opportunities such as conferences that I could speak at, but that it would also help me connect with the right people who would provide me a way to make inroads to achieve those professional goals. On the other hand, it could only notify me of the professional opportunities. It could not act on them in any way. It has always been my choice as to whether or not I will follow through on an opportunity. The consequences of achieving this result is that I would travel more, write more, or get involved in networking events, all of which I felt were acceptable consequences.

After you've determined the goal and results, you need to develop a statement of intent. The statement of intent summarizes what the entity will do, setting the intention for it. Think of the statement of intent as the core programming of the entity. For the opportunity the statement of intent was: "Find professional opportunities and connections for me and make me aware of them."

After you come up with the statement of intent, you will want to include details about the general and specific realms of influence the entity draws. A realm of influence could be a planetary or elemental energy, or a specific attribute, emotion, or behavior that the entity draws upon. My opportunity entity draws on the planetary energy of Mercury for information and connections, as well as the energy of networking.

Next, you need to come up with the name of the entity. One approach to developing the name involves getting rid of the repeating letters in your statement of intent and taking whatever letters are left and developing a name from them. Another method I've used is to simply come up with an atypical name that stands out and is different from what you'd usually hear. I named my opportunity entity Cerontis.

Appearance is the next detail. What does your entity look like? It can look like a human, animal, plant, or some blend or something else altogether, but ideally what it looks like will help with how it achieves its job. In the case of Cerontis, it has an appearance of a plant with vines and webs. It uses both aspects to discover opportunities and determine if they are appropriate ones to notify me of.

Housing is the physical home of the entity. I find it useful to combine the appearance of the entity with the housing. Housing can be anything you create or make. You could sculpt a statue, draw or paint a picture of the entity. I choose to paint my entities. The creativity you apply to the creation of the entity is part of how you charge it with the intent and goals you want it to accomplish. You don't need to be a gifted artist either. I am not a professional painter and I doubt my paintings would appear in an art gallery, but for the purposes of my spiritual work, they suffice.

You also need to determine what will be used to feed your entity. Even if it isn't a living being in the conventional sense of the word, you are bringing it to life and you need to find a way to sustain it without having it draw on your own energy. I recommend feeding it via the very activities it performs. Cerontis is fed by the opportunities I choose to explore. This consequently has helped it become more accurate, because its life is reliant upon my choice to follow through on its recommendations.

The next detail to focus on is describing what the magical powers of the entity are. You may have already done this, but it doesn't hurt to get specific about it. You want to describe what the entity actually does, and how it does it. In the case of Cerontis, it scans imaginary time to discover specific possibilities that represent opportunities that I'd like to know more about it. It then informs me of those opportunities via my intuition. It also manipulates the field of probabilities to make it easier for me to follow through on those opportunities by helping me find the right people to connect with.

Everything I've described above are the essential elements involved in creating an entity. There are additional details you can include, such as activating the entity during a specific planetary hour or associating colors and scents with it, but in my opinion these are optional features that are only necessary if you think they will help you activate the entity.

In a very real sense all of the details you have filled out have already helped you create the entity. When you create the housing for the entity, visualize it coming to life with each stroke of the brush or movement of your hands on clay. You are giving it life so that it in term can fulfill its function in your life. Think of it performing its function as well as the results it will achieve. Once you've finished the housing you've activated the entity and it can perform its task.

Don't expect instant results once you activate it. However within a short time (a couple weeks at most) you should know if it is producing the desired results. If it isn't producing the desired results, I suggest looking over your notes to determine if you left a detail out or were too specific. Correcting information usually gets the entity on task and performing to your expectations.

There is one other thing I'd like to mention. I only create an entity when I feel it can perform a function or task that I couldn't perform easily or at all. I don't create one when I can do something myself. Creating and working with entities can be a very useful form of magic, but what makes them most effective is doing something you couldn't easily do on your own. For example, I can scan the field of probabilities and access opportunities, but it would take a lot more work and time than I want to put toward it. Creating an entity to perform that function has automated that need and allows me to focus my time and efforts on the pursuits I am focused on.

There are two other types of entities you can also draw on for help: corporate and pop culture entities.

Corporate Entities

Corporations create entities all the time. In fact, your average corporation is an entity in and of itself. Think of a particular brand and what do you think of? You might think of a slogan or an image or even a song. For example, when you think of Nike you probably think of the swoosh and the phrase "Just do it". Or if you think of Intel you might think of the color blue, and the Intel song. We are bombarded everyday with corporate culture images and sounds, but we can actually use those images and sounds to our own advantage.

Corporate entities already exist, so when you work with one you are interacting with an existing entity. To work with it you want to use corporate logos, branding, phrases, imagery, and sounds to help you make a connection. To go back to the Nike example, you would use the image of the swoosh, the phrase "just do it" and you might also use images of athletes playing sports while wearing the Nike shoes, as well as a pair of Nike shoes that you wear.

The reasons you'll work with a corporate entity usually involve helping you to find a job or to advance in your current job. In the Career chapter, I'll describe how to do this in further detail, but for now keep in mind that while a corporate entity can be a useful ally in helping you find a job or advance in your career, its goal is to pursue profit for the company. It isn't looking out for you out of any sense of goodness, but rather because you are considered to be part of the corporation. In addition, a corporate entity will pursue its own interests, up to and including trying to influence you to buy the products or services of the company.

With that said a corporate entity can be a useful ally and in the next chapter we'll cover the different ways it can help you with your career.

Pop Culture Entities

Pop culture entities are not necessarily corporate entities. Pop culture entities are entities that are created from whatever is considered popular within a given culture, but can also be created by what is considered relevant in your life[3]. A pop culture entity can be a corporate entity, but it could also be a

---

[3] I describe different types of pop culture entities in more depth in Pop Culture Magick and Multi-Media Magic.

cartoon character, a persona of a famous person, or a character from a book or film. For example, if I wanted to work with a pop culture entity of investing, I'd work with Warren Buffet. The pop culture entity of Warren Buffet isn't the actual person who is known as Warren Buffet, but rather the investment persona that Warren Buffet (and others) has created.

Pop culture entities can make it easier for you work with an existing concept such as investment, while using something familiar to you that others will also recognize. Additionally, pop culture entities can apply to a variety of other aspects of wealth such as health, money management, love, networking, business, etc.

Pop culture entities are similar to corporate entities (and deities for that matter) in that they have their own interests, which may or may not conflict with yours. It is important to pick your pop culture entities carefully, and you may even want to be selective in what you draw on when you work with a pop culture entity. I work with Billy Blanks (the inventor of Tae Bo) as an exercise entity. The pop culture persona I work with is filtered in that I'm working with an entity that feels passionate about exercise, but I've filtered out the actual spiritual beliefs that Billy Blanks has, because those beliefs are incompatible with mine, and I don't want that influence in my life.

This chapter has introduced you to different types of entities you can work with. In later chapters I will provide detailed examples of how to work with these types of entities in wealth magic. Entities and Deities can be powerful allies that help you accomplish your magical goals and make your mundane life easier. It is important to treat them with respect and honor your end of any deal you create with them. Even if it is an entity that you've created, you still need to honor what you've promised to provide it. You are creating and maintaining a relationship that can have a profound impact on your life for better or worse.

Conclusion

Working with deities and entities can provide you valuable allies and resources to help you achieve your wealth goals. As with anything else related to wealth, they should be employed strategically and properly compensated for their efforts.

Chapter 6: Wealth Magic for Career Success

There are two types of career magic a person typically uses. The first type involves utilizing magic to find a career. The second type involves utilizing magic to do well at your career and ideally to get a raise/promotion. There is one very important caveat that needs to be raised before we can discuss the magical work any further. Career magic is only effective if you are also already doing everything else you'd be doing in a mundane situation without magic. What makes career magic effective is that it stacks the deck in your favor. Just doing magic to get a career or promotion doesn't work if you aren't doing any activities that would make it possible for you to get the career or the promotion. There are no free handouts in the universe, and to expect that a career will just land in your lap or that a promotion will be handed to you without doing any work on your part is unrealistic.

I also want to comment on the difference between a job and a career. A career is an investment in doing something you enjoy. When you work in a career you are planning on being in that career for the long haul. You may change companies or even go off on your own, but what you are doing is part of your calling. A job is different. A job is something you take because you either don't know what you really want to do or don't believe you can make a career out of doing what you love. You take a job to pay bills and bring home a paycheck.

In my opinion, it's better to get paid to do what you love to do and make a career out of it. I won't say it's always easy and you may find that you need to hold down a daytime job while pursuing your career, but settling for a job goes against what wealth magic is about. Wealth magic, as it applies to the work you do, is about doing work you love. Doing work you love feeds your sense of self-worth and motivates you to enjoy your life, while working at a job tends to deaden people and make them feel unsatisfied with their lives.

In that vein of thought, the focus of this chapter is to help you find a career as opposed to finding a job. You can still apply these techniques toward finding a job, but why would you really want to, if you know it won't bring you the sense of satisfaction that you know you deserve?

Career Hunting

Hunting for a career, or more specifically your next position in your career, can be time consuming and demoralizing if you aren't currently working. And if you are working, it can still be stressful, especially as you try to make time to find your next position while still working at the previous one. Often what holds a person back from finding their next position is the inevitable doubts and insecurities that arise when the next position isn't found right away. You can literally spend months, if not even longer, career hunting.

However magic can take the stress of career hunting and turn it into a tool for your advantage. All the emotions you feel are reactions to the stress of the situation, but they are also energy in motion, and career hunting in general is really an activity of movement. When you are hunting for a career or your next position in a career you open yourself up to the possibility of movement. The key is to actually allow yourself to trust that movement and harness it as part of both the magical and mundane process of getting the next position in your career.

The movement manifests through the activities you do to hunt for a career. When you create or revise your resume or fill out an application or write a cover letter you are generating movement toward finding your next career. When you search for positions on sites such as Linkedin, Monster or Career Builder you are generating movement. When you make phone calls, go to interviews and write thank you notes you are generating movement. All of that movement builds up the potential for you to find a career. And when you apply magic to that movement you stack the odds in your favor and build up enough momentum to reach a tipping point that puts the momentum of the universe in your favor and aligns you with your next career.

That is the mindset I've always applied when I hunted for my next career position, and it always worked. That mindset is a magical tool in and of itself because it creates a particular view of reality, which perceives every activity you do as one that has direct meaning and power applied to your career hunt. When you filter reality in that way, it allows you to generate momentum toward finding your career, as well as allowing you to trust the magic and feed whatever doubts you feel into the process.

To create this mindset, I create a sigil that represents the career hunt. The sigil embodies the mindset, but it also performs one additional function. It takes all of the emotions you feel about the career hunt and turns those emotions into fuel for the mindset. Every time you feel depressed, frustrated, stressed, excited or happy in regards to the career hunt, the energy of those emotions is fed into the career hunt to help move it toward its ultimate conclusion: you working in your next career position.

The sigil is a symbol that represents your ideal position, salary, benefits, etc. Before you create it, take a moment to list the kind of position you are looking for and what kind of pay you are looking for, as well as benefits. Also describe your ideal working environment. What does it look like? What are your fellow employees like? How well do you get along with the management? What will you do in this position? How much will you enjoy it? Finally, make sure you also include what you don't want in your work environment, both in terms of types of people you work with, as well as anything else that would detract from your enjoyment of your career.

Taking your time to answer these questions can help you paint a picture of your career and allow you to develop a sigil that represents what you are looking for. The sigil can be drawn, but I preferred to paint my career sigils, in order to fully express the answers to the questions above, as well as capture the emotional and career hunting energy that will be used fuel the sigil. The sigil is fired every time you do a career hunting activity, such as networking or filling out an application. At the same time those activities also charge the sigil up, so that it can be fired again when you do your next career hunting activity. This allows you to turn the movement of your career hunting activity into a tipping point that puts the momentum of the universe behind your efforts.

An alternate approach to this working involves creating an entity that helps you with your career hunt. The example below illustrates how such an entity can work.

The Creation of Good Job

When Kat, my wife, first moved up to Portland, she moved away from a stable job in California. She had a couple connections, which helped her meet some contacts in her desired career field, but she also encountered a lot of difficulty in landing a position. Part of it was that she was hunting for a career during a down economy in a place where she only had a couple connections, and part of it was that although she had over 19 years of experience in her career field, the companies she was looking to be hired by were looking for professionals just out of college (who wouldn't want as much money).

We knew it wouldn't be an easy career hunt, and on top of that she was going through other life changes that made it hard for her to focus on using magic directly to find a position. So we decided to create an entity that could help her find her new career position. The entity could focus on her career hunt full time while she made a consistent effort to find work, but also focused on the other life changes she was dealing with.

The entity had several functions. First, it would help her find the career she was looking for, at the salary level she requested, and with the benefits she wanted. Second it would help her find the right people to connect with so that she could advance in her career. Finally, it'd offer intuitive pings for situations where she might need to take a course of action. The reason we created the entity with these specifications is because we recognized that she'd want to advance in her career. As it turned out, it was good that we added those features.

The entity was fed by the career hunting and networking activities my wife did. Every time she filled out an application or went in for an interview, the entity was fed. At the same time it worked to get her interviews. We created the entity in August of 2010 and within a couple weeks she'd landed an interview for a position she wanted. She didn't get that position, although she got a part time job as a trainer. However in mid-October, the company unexpectedly had an opening for the same position she'd applied for in August, and she got that position. My wife landed a temporary position, which meant that she'd lose the position when the contract ended the following June.

However Good Job was working, not only in terms of helping her find a position and the desired salary, but also helping her network with the right people while she was employed at the company. Thanks to the connections she made and the continual work that Good Job performed, after she lost the position that June, she landed a better paying position a month later. She received a raise and a promotion in the span of less than a year. A lot of it was due to her hard work, but Good Job played its part by helping her be in the right place at the right time. Since that time, she's continued to get access to the right people and be in the right situations for future advancement.

Some Further Considerations about Entity Work

My wife and I created Good Job because she had a lot going on in her life, and even now I'd say it was wise choice because in her current position she is very busy. Having an entity manage the career advancement part of her career and guide her efforts has been useful for her, and also allows her to focus on the other aspects of her career, which in turn enhances career advancement opportunities

I don't think creating an entity is necessarily superior to doing career hunting magic yourself, but there is something to be said for creating such an entity with a proactive approach to career hunting and advancement. Typically, career hunting magic is performed in order to help you get the next position, and then the enchantment is done. You've found the next position, you are getting paid and you have benefits and that is that. In a way, the typical career hunting magic is reactive magic, done mainly as a reaction to your unemployment or your desire to get out of a position you don't want to be in anymore. The same can also be said of most career advancement magic. The magic is done to get a single promotion or raise, but once that short-term goal is accomplished, the magic is finished, and the magician becomes complacent. The beauty of Good Job is that while it was created for the short-term goal of helping my wife land a position at a new company, it was also designed with long term goals in mind. It is an entity that my wife will work with until she decides to retire, and even then she might take it with her to her next career. She'll never need to do a career hunting spell because the entity will take care of all that for her.

The lesson to take away from all of this is that often times when a person practices magic for practical solutions; s/he does it as a reaction to a problem and focuses on the immediate need as opposed to the long-term need. I think it is better to be proactive in your application of magic to your life. Sometimes that can involve practical magic that you do directly, and sometimes it can involve the creation of an entity that handles the magical end of things for the long term. It's up to you to determine what type of magic you'll use to help you resolve a problem, but think beyond the immediate problem. Focus on the long-term implications and see what you can do to leverage those implications in your favor.

If I was still in the corporate world, I would create a career hunting entity like Good Job for similar purposes as opposed to doing direct practical magic myself. Having done direct practical magic in the past to land a position, I can say that my own focus was on the short term. It was more important to land a position, but once I had I didn't think of the long-term goals. In wealth magic, we always want to think of the long term as well as the short term. If we focus only on the short term, we are merely surviving.

Career Success and Advancement Magic

The key to success in your career ultimately lies in how you to choose show up in your career. If you are someone who is content to do only what is asked of you, and not give any more effort than that, you're chances of getting a raise or promotion are slim. In fact, if what I just wrote describes you I suggest spending some time considering what it is you really want to do, because chances are you are just working at a job as opposed to a career that energizes and excites you. A career should make you want to be ambitious because you love what you are doing and you want to learn more and challenge yourself.

If you do enjoy your career and you want to challenge yourself, consider the following mundane advice as it will help any magical work you do. How are you showing up at your work place? Are you dressing like everyone else or are you making an effort to tidy your appearance up? While appearance isn't the sole evaluator for workplace performance, people do pay attention to how you appear. While dressing in blue jeans like everyone else may make you feel like part of the crowd, it could be worthwhile to dress up in dress slacks and a business shirt. It shows you mean business and that you want to be taken seriously.

Much more important than appearance is your actual performance. What are you doing to go above and beyond the actual level of work you need to do? While it's easy to just do the level of work required, if you want a raise and/or promotion you need to be willing to do more than the bare minimum. Ask your manager or boss if there are other activities you can do and then do those activities and ask for more. This shows self-initiative on your part and indicates that you can handle more responsibility. Remember that if you want the raise or promotion, you need to actually demonstrate that you can earn it.

Networking is also another activity that can help you move ahead in your career. Spend time with your manager and cultivate a good relationship with him or her. Ask questions at meetings and show interest in what other people on your team are doing. Also find out who the movers and shakers of the company and industry are and start following them via social media. If you can comment on their blog or social media updates go ahead and do that. The relationships you build can prove helpful to you because the people you know will advocate for you. By developing a strong network you will have people who will back you up and look out for you.

All of those activities are mundane, but all of them have value for your magical efforts, because they improve the possibility that you will get a raise/promotion. If you are known as a reliable worker who has good connections and is willing to take on more responsibilities. It makes the process of getting a raise much easier than if you do the bare minimum and don't have strong relationships with your manager and other people who hold positions of power in the company.

Another thing you want to do is keep a documented record of your activities. This is useful because when you have an interview with your manager you can provide proof about what you've done that demonstrates why you deserve a raise or promotion. At the same time you should be humble enough to also seek his/her advice on what you can do to improve your job performance. Suggesting to your manager that you would like to know what you can improve, as well as setting goals, will go a long way to show that you are invested in your career and want to provide your best effort to your company.

However, it is also good to know when to employ magic to help you with your job performance. I've used magic several times to make the work I was doing easier, or the manager I was dealing with more manageable on my end. My first technical writing job at Boeing was an excellent example of using magic to make the job easier. I did two magical workings and both of them helped me immensely with the job and my manager.

Both of these workings happened at the same job (and it was a job as opposed to a career). I'd gotten hired as a technical writer at Boeing, but I didn't have much experience doing technical writing. My manager had a temper and wasn't good at managing his employees, so he wasn't too thrilled to have a wet behind the ears tech writer. When I had been working there for only a month or so he told me that the writing and work needed to be improved or I'd be let go of. I couldn't afford that, so I went into action.

My first action was to create an energetic buffer in my manager's office that would dampen his temper. I created energetic constructs in his office when he wasn't there. Those energetic buffers siphoned his emotional energy, particularly when he was getting bad tempered. Shortly after I put the energetic constructs into his office, everyone noticed that he became a lot mellower. I did energy work to create to create the constructs. Essentially I created energy pillows and put them on the corners of his office. Whenever his temper started to rise the pillows would gather the emotions and soften them.

While creating the energetic buffer was useful, I did want to do a better job and I realized that while part of my problem involved mastering technical writing, part of it also involved understanding the technology. The project I was working on had an acronym that represented it. I decided to use that acronym to connect with the spirit or entity of the project and ask it to help me understand the technology better, as well as write better. The entity was very willing to help because it recognized that the work I was doing was integral to its manifestation as a physical reality.

I recognize that many magicians wouldn't think that a project they were working on had a spirit associated with it, but I figured that the project was more than just work we were doing. What we were doing involved the manifestation of the project as a viable technology interface. All that work we were putting into the project created a spirit that I could interact with. I had no trouble contacting that spirit and it was easy to get it to help me, because it saw the benefit. Shortly after I contacted it, my technical writing skills improved and I also picked up the technology much quicker. A month after that I was on good terms with my manager, and for the remaining time I worked at Boeing I had no further issues with anyone.

At subsequent tech writing jobs I employed the same methods to make my work at those jobs go smoothly. With each manager I created the appropriate energetic construct that would keep him/her low maintenance and easy to work for. I also worked with the spirit of whatever project I was working on, which made each project easier, because I had the spiritual support of the project. You could take this one step further and work with the spirit of the company. The only problem I found with that approach is that the spirit of the company is too broad. While it may be interested in helping you do a better job, it's not going to help you focus in the same way that the spirit of the project will help you. I'd suggest working with the spirit of your company for situations where you want to network with people that are higher up than you. The company spirit/entity will help you with this process as long as you are working in its best interests.

I'll admit that my approach to corporate magic had less to do with career advancement and more to do with making my job easier to do. Those two purposes can go hand in hand, so the workings I did could be used to help you advance in your career. But the workings can be simply used to make the work easier. In my case, I didn't see technical writing as a career. I got out of it as soon as I could, but it was a useful short-term job I could do, while I figured out what I really wanted to do with my life.

If you are in the career you want to be in, then these techniques can help you stand out if combined with the mundane activities I mentioned above. Also if you want to cultivate a deeper connection to the spirit of the company it could be useful to create a little altar to the company in your office space. And best of all, the altar can be put in plain site without arousing any suspicions on the part of your co-workers. After all, if you choose to show just how committed you are to the company by having company regalia and artifacts on your desk, who is going to really question it?

Most companies will have mugs made, or calendars, or even little statues made. Additionally you can easily get t-shirts and other apparel to wear that embodies the company spirit and shows your pride in working at the company. For example, at Boeing it was very easy to get mugs, model planes, calendars etc., with the company logo and products prominently displayed. And you can get shirts to wear. The shirts become your ritual garb for the workplace, while the other material is used to create the altar. Set aside a part of your desk that will strictly be dedicated to the spirit of the company. Place any artifacts in that area. For example, you could hang your company calendar there, as well as a picture of the company product. You might also have a mug that you placed there or whatever else you find that embodies the spirit of the company. All of those artifacts can be dedicated to the spirit of the company and used to commune with it, as well as show your dedication to it. Each day before you start work, clean the altar and the items on it. The act of cleaning is your time to connect with the spirit of the company. You might also take a moment to briefly meditate about your day and what you will do throughout the day. Visualize every single activity you will do and imprint the company logo on top of those activities, syncing the work you do with the logo of the company. By doing this you will align yourself with the favor of the company's spirit and put it on your side, working in your favor. The best devotion you can show is to do your work well and if you feel ambitious find ways to advance your career.

Conclusion

Being in a career you enjoy is a form of wealth in and of itself. The enrichment you feel as a result of doing work that is rewarding is important to acknowledge. As I said at the beginning of the chapter, it's better to find and advance in a career you enjoy instead of working in a job you hate. I say that from experience. Working at a job you don't enjoy can suck a lot of the joy and creativity from your life. The work you do should enliven and challenge you to grow. If it doesn't do that, even if it helps you pay the bills, it's killing your life. It is important to pay your bills, but it's better to find something you genuinely enjoy doing so that you get more out of it than just money. After all, you are spending a significant chunk of your life at work.

If you are hunting for a job, don't just rely on the online sites such as montser.com. You can usually find networking events that are specifically for job hunters, and there are other resources available if you do a bit of research. For example, in Oregon there are several career centers that teach people job skills and show them how to get and keep work. If you go to a networking event you can ask people there for job hunting resources and they can point you in the right direction.

If you find that working for a company doesn't bring you joy, then, like me, you may need to explore self-employment to find your career. Self-employment has its own challenges, but the rewards are well worth the challenges, as we'll explore further in chapter 7.

Chapter 7: Business Magic

Owning a business can be simultaneously one of the most rewarding and frustrating experiences you undergo. It's rewarding because you get to make the rules and your schedule is determined by yourself for the most part. It's frustrating because you only get paid if you get results, and you have to do a lot of activities that aren't directly related to income but nonetheless are essential for making sure that your business is successful. When you are a business owner you wear many hats that you didn't need to wear when you worked at a company.

For most people running a business starts out as a part time side career that is used to supplement daytime work and is done because the person sees an opportunity to turn a talent or hobby into a business. However, a business can quickly take on a life of its own and can make a lot of demands on the available time you have for other areas of your life. At the same time, leaving the relative safety of a full time position with a stable salary and benefits can seem threatening, especially when you consider that owning a business doesn't provide the same benefits or definite salary that your day time work may offer you. Owning a business is an adventure, but it is also a lot of hard work, and you may not have a lot of profit the first few years of owning the business. Anyone who is truly successful with their own business will tell you that it took years of effort to reach the success they now have.

The reality of owning a business is also important to consider. You may think initially that you can set your own schedule or do everything the way you want to, or that you'll get to spend lots of time doing the work that you want to do, but the reality is that owning a business calls on you to do more than just be a technician, and it also can eat up a lot of your schedule. You may love to bake, make art or offer healing services, but unless you know how to work on your business, your passion will burn out and you will find yourself working for someone else once again. Learning how to work on a business means learning how to delegate work you don't want to do to people who can do it, while also taking on certain roles that every business owner has to take on: marketing, networking, leading, etc. These roles are essential to the success of the business, but most new business owners don't fully recognize just how much work is involved until after they've owned the business for a while.

My point in writing all of this isn't to discourage you from owning your own business. Rather I want to help you make an informed choice as well as look at how wealth magic can make the process easier for you in both the short and long term. My own journey as a business owner has been an eventful one, but also very rewarding.

Exercise: Meditation on Why You Want to be a Business Owner

Understanding what motivates you to be self-employed can be helpful for determining if you can make it as a business owner. Sometimes, when your business is floundering, the only way you'll stay motivated is by drawing on the reasons that made you go into business for yourself in the first place. The following questions are worth meditating on:

1. Why do you want to be self-employed? How would being self-employed benefit yourself and how would it benefit your clientele?

2. Are you able to maintain self-discipline and work on your business?

3. What is the worst thing that could happen if your business doesn't work out? What will happen to you if your business does work out?

4. How much money do you want to make? How much do you want to charge for your services?

Answer each of these questions and then meditate on your answers. With the questions on number 3, it may be useful to do a pathworking and actually visualize what it would like if you failed or were highly successful. Note any feelings that come up for you as you answer these questions. For example, if you feel fear around how much you'll charge for your services, you'll want to explore that fear in depth, because you will need to set a price and stick with it if you want to get paid. Use these questions as a guide to help you understand your initial feelings around being self-employed, but don't let the answers discourage you either. If you truly want to own your own business you will find a way to work through any internal barriers that come up.

My Journey as a Business Owner

I first discovered my love of small business as a teenager, when I'd help my mom vend at art fairs and also help her package orders. It gave me a taste of what being a small business owner was, but it wasn't until much later that I really discovered it.

In 2004, I published my first book at Immanion Press and shortly after ended up creating and managing the non-fiction imprint. I didn't and don't own Immanion Press, but I still learned a lot about running a business because I got involved on every level. Not only was I an author (which in itself is a business), but I was an editor who handled acquisitions as well as all levels of the editing process. Eventually I learned how to do layout design, and I also helped broker distribution deals. Storm Constantine (the owner of Immanion Press) eventually brought me in on the top level decisions that involved running the business. I am not the owner of the company, but I help run the company and make decisions that affect the direction the company goes in.

And as I mentioned earlier I became an author. Being an author has always been a business. You don't just write a book. You market and promote it. You do workshops and book signings, teach classes, and do whatever else you can to sell books. Actually you do more than sell books. You sell yourself to some degree. I'm selling my expertise, and books are just one form of selling that expertise. In 2013 I started the Way of the Magician Mystery School, which has allowed me to create classes around my books and is already becoming a second viable business alongside my primary business.

I started my primary business (Imagine Your Reality

Business Coaching) in April of 2008. It was initially a part time business, while I worked full time as a technical writer. My technical writer contract ended in August of 2008 right before the economy crashed, and I couldn't find work, so suddenly my coaching business was full time. I chose to focus on offering social media services because it seemed like the one service anyone was willing to spend money on. I continued offering social media services until December of 2011 and my business gradually grew, but it took a lot of work and I made a lot of mistakes along the way. In December of 2011, I changed my business from social media to business coaching. I had made a promise to myself that I would get out of technology and at that time I finally felt it was the right time to leave social media behind.

Currently I'm a business coach in Imagine Your Reality, while Magical Experiments is my spiritual coaching/author business. I work on both of them full time, and while both are a lot of work, I am happier than I have ever been. Because I rebranded Imagine Your Reality, that business started back at square one, but in one year it is already growing and I'm using my prior experience as a social media consultant to help that growth occur faster. The Magical Experiments business is also growing and morphing into the Way of the Magician Mystery School. And my prior experiences with owning a business or helping run one have helped immensely.

These paragraphs don't begin to fully convey my story as a business owner, but you can probably tell that a lot has happened on my journey. What I haven't told you is all the work that has gone into marketing my businesses, or all the networking events I've attended, or classes I've taken, or the meetings I've had with prospects, or the time I spend doing the books for my businesses. Owning a business is a lot of work, but it is also a lot of fun. If you don't own a business, but think you might want to, or you own a part or full time business, you'll get a lot from this chapter, but most of all remember that owning a business isn't like working in a job. When you work at a job you are paid for your time. When you are a business you are only paid if you get results. In that sense, owning a business is a lot like being a magician. The results define the success of the business (or your magical work).

As a business coach I advise my clients on how to work on their businesses, instead of in them, as well as how to grow the business successfully. A lot of my work involves helping them recognize how to delegate work to other people, whether employees or a vendor who is better able to accomplish the task. At the same time, I'd also say that it's equally important to know when to bring magic into the mix of your business, as well as how to apply it. We'll start at the most obvious place: your business plan.

Business Plan Magic

If you don't have a business plan for your business, you need to write one. It doesn't need to be a formal business plan that you'd present to a bank to get a loan, but it does need to be a plan that helps you understand how you will grow your business. In fact, I'd say that the formal business plan is a separate document altogether, because even though it may provide information on what you plan to do to grow the business, it's a plan based on having a loan. That can be useful and we'll touch on some magic you can do to help you get the loan, but I also think you should have a separate business plan that strictly focuses on the actions you will take to grow your business.

Your business action plan is the plan that provides details about the actions you'll take over three years within specific time increments. It's a plan you will look over frequently and use as guidance, though not to the point that you can't adapt to changing circumstances. And writing up this plan is a form of magic in and of itself. It takes all the thoughts in your head and turns them into an objective record of what you are doing to grow your business and how you are going to do it. That act of writing is a form of manifestation and it provides structure for your business as an entity, as well as how your business will fit into your life.

The specific time increments of the plan will be three months, six months, one year, two years and three years. You are allowed to be vague for the second and third year, but you should have very specific action steps developed for three months through a year. You will also have specific categories for this business action plan. These categories are below, along with a brief explanation for the category:

Expertise: Your expertise is the service or product you provide. It is something you ideally do because you love to do it. In order to own a business you need to have a service or product to provide people. However, just having a service or product isn't enough, which is why other skills are included below.

Marketing: This is the ability to identify your target market, as well as power partners (people who offer complementary service and products, but who aren't in competition with you). Beyond identifying your target market, you need to also explain the value and benefits of what you offer (i.e. why should they choose you over your competition) in their language, which means using as little technical jargon as possible, and doing your best to understand why your target clientele want what they want.

Finances: Your business is defined by your cashflow and your ability to manage your finances, which includes doing the books (or hiring someone to do them for you), paying taxes, and projecting where your business will be and how you'll use your financial resources to grow the business. Your financial attitude is also an important element that needs to be considered, because of how it can impact your business.

Operations/Process: This involves learning how to work on your business. A business owner needs to develop processes and policies for working on the business, including communication policies, payment policies, how problems are handled, and doing the necessary admin work that every business owner needs to do.

Technology: Technology doesn't just refer to technology that you'd learn in your field of expertise, but also to any other technology you need to use in order to run your business. It is important for the business owner to keep up with the technological demands on business. The social media revolution provides plenty of case studies of how technology can impact business, as well as why it's important to keep up with the technology.

Leadership: Even if you are the only employee in your business, you still need to know how to lead yourself. If you do have actual employees, you also need to know how to lead them. Beyond that, when you are a business owner, you are usually involved in your community and becoming a leader also involves leading the community around you.

Work-Life Balance: It is all too easy to become a workaholic when you own a business. Learning to cultivate work-life balance helps you know when to turn off the computer, punch the clock and take time for yourself and your family. Work-life balance is essential for renewal, which is the process of making time for yourself to recharge and rejuvenate, so that you can approach your business with a fresh and focused outlook.

Attitude: Attitude describes the emotional core of your business. It's what motivates you to own the business and what motivates you to keep at it even and especially on the days when you feel overwhelmed and frustrated.

Customer Service: Ideally your customers are happy with you and your services/products, but you want to keep them happy, which means developing not only problem response strategies, while continuing conversations and rapport with your customers. You want them to know that you are always thinking of them.

Employee Satisfaction: Are your employees happy? If you don't have employees, are you happy with you as a boss? Knowing how to keep employees happy and buying into the company vision is important to the success of the business. It also can tell you a lot about the culture of your company.

Sales: How many sales do you want? How will you get those sales and how often do you need to go out and make a sale? How do your sales fit into your financial strategy for your business? Sales isn't the same as marketing because it involves closing the deal. Marketing explains why someone should buy from you, while sales closes the deal and sustains your business.

Networking: Are you connected to the right people? Networking focuses on helping you develop a support network that allows you to refer business to other professionals, while also getting business referrals from them. However, networking is also about mentor relationships, and the ability to listen, ask questions, and give to other people.

These brief descriptions provide you an idea of the actual tasks involved in running a business. It seems like a lot to do, and in fact it is a lot to do. A business owner wears many hats, and it's fair to say that owning a business and actually providing the service or product are two full time jobs. Magic can help you manage some of these details, but the reality ultimately is that making a business successful is up to you and your willingness to take action on a consistent basis.

Writing a business plan is one of the first steps you can take toward making your business a successful reality. I see writing as a magical act because it takes the concept you have in your head and begins the process of manifestation. When you write something down you are creating an objective record and reality, separate from the thoughts in your head. A written business plan is the objective record of what you will do to grow your business and a potent act of magic because it describes the life of your business as well as the actions that will be taken to sustain that life.

As I mentioned above you'll take each of these categories and write about the actions you will take in three months, six months, etc. Be as specific as possible, especially for the first year. I suggest reviewing your written business plan every three months. You want to do this so that you can determine if you are accomplishing your actions, but also so that you can change your plan to adapt to the changes that have occurred in your business and life. It's important to remember that your business plan isn't written in stone. It is a plan of action, but it is also a plan that can and should be changed as needed so that you can make your business successful.

If you want to add more overt forms of magic to your business plan, you could create a sigil that represents the business plan and put it on the written document. The sigil's purpose should be to keep you on task and focused on accomplishing your business activities. It should be tied to the plan so that when you change the plan, you also change the sigil. In one sense your business plan is the programming language of the sigil. The sigil is the magical force applied to keep you on task, while the plan is the description of what the sigil needs to put in front of you to make sure you do the task. I've created just such a sigil for my business plan and it's helped me by keeping me focused on the high priority items on the action plan, while also providing me awareness about resources I can use to help me accomplish the actions I need to do to manifest the plan into reality.

If you do create a business plan to get a loan you can also integrate a sigil into that plan, but make sure that you put it on a copy of the plan as opposed to the copy you'll take into the bank. You might consider your home copy, your master copy, which the sigil is implanted into so that it can influence any other copies of the business plan that other people are looking at. I'd also suggest keeping copies of your business plans (both the action and loan plan) on your wealth magic altar, so that they can be charged, and even so that you look at them each day to remind yourself of what you will do to grow your business.

The Archetype of a Business Owner

When you think of a business owner, what is the first image that comes to mind? Do you think of an immoral person who runs a corporation and doesn't care how his/her actions affect others (like Lex Luthor or the leadership of Enron), or do you think of the business owner as someone who cares about his/her employees as well as the customer experience that people have (such as the leadership of Zappo's)? The image of a business owner that may come to mind might also be the owner of a small shop down the street or people meeting at a networking event.

Unfortunately in pop culture, what we typically see is a distorted version of the business owner, someone who is corrupt, only looking out for his/her own interests. Such a character is seen as greedy, hedonistic, dishonest, and always obsessed with business. The business owner is often portrayed as a villain in pop culture.

The reality is a different matter altogether. To be a

successful business owner you can't be a Lex Luthor, and the majority of business owners aren't motivated by greed or a desire for money. What they are really motivated by is a desire to live by their own rules, work on what they truly feel passionate about, and have the freedom to work with who they want to work with. Being a business owner can be hard work, but the reward is that you truly get to be independent and live life on your own terms.

Being a successful business owner does involve recognizing the role you play in the community at large. The success of a business is reliant upon the clients the business has, and a business owner needs to be involved in the community and show interest in his/her clients. In truth, a business owner needs to think of how the community perceives his/her actions. A business owner needs to be honest and to build trust and all of that can be lost if s/he says the wrong or chooses to be dishonest.

Business owners are usually involved in their communities. For example, I belong to a number of community organizations and I regularly participate in meetings for those organizations, helping to make the organization and its contribution to the community more successful with my own contributions. Indeed, it is fair to say that that part of business success is based on choosing to contribute to the community. Many business owners I know are involved with at least one or two professional organizations and are usually involved in those organizations on some level beyond just showing up to networking meetings. They also tend to be the more successful business owners, because the community recognizes their efforts and wants to support them in kind.

A business owner also needs to think of the quality of services and products s/he provides, as well as how on time s/he is with the delivery of said products and services. The cliche of under promise and over deliver is an apt description of the expectations that every business owner faces, in that the business owner must show that s/he can deliver on his/her promises, and if s/he is doing business right s/he is providing higher value than s/he promised. The value of what you provide is what defines the reputation of your business. Your ability to focus your business on the needs and problems of your clients is more important than anything else. Can you solve the problems that your clients have and do you solve those problems better than someone else?

Whatever you envision a business owner to be, think carefully as to whether that vision is accurate or how you want to show up as, as a business owner. If it isn't, then you want to revise that vision accordingly. What are the ideal characteristics of a successful business person? How does the successful business person manifest those characteristics in his/her life? You may find it useful to draw on real life examples of people you know or follow to provide inspiration and spiritual mentorship. For example, a few business people I am inspired by are Mark LeBlanc, C. Richard Weylman, and Lee Cockerell. You may or may not recognize these names. They aren't famous in the way that Warren Buffet or Bill Gates are, but you don't need to draw on super famous people to discover successful business owners. A successful business owner that you draw inspiration from could be someone you know or the author of a book you've read. Whoever s/he is, a good question to ask is: What attributes or behaviors do I admire, and what would I want to incorporate into my archetype of a business owner?

My archetype of a business owner, which essentially is my idealized version of myself as a business owner, has the following behavioral traits: he is disciplined, creative, innovative, punctual, attentive, compassionate, caring, able to see the big picture and focus in on details, charismatic, friendly, intelligent, quick, perceptive, etc. The list could go on and on because there are so many traits I want to draw on, and I'm always keeping myself open to discovering how I could be a better business person.

One exercise that I've developed and found useful for developing the archetype of the business owner both for myself and my clients involves creating a slogan that represents your attitude, and then a list of ten qualities you'd like to take out into the world every day. My slogan is "Go in for the win" My qualities include creativity, flexibility, and persistence, and beside each quality I write a one sentence explanation of what that quality means to me and how I plan to manifest it in my everyday life. I read this list each day to help keep me sharp and focused on what I really want to bring into my business.

Taylor Ellwood

Occasionally I'll change the list if I feel a need to focus on integrating a quality into my life that isn't on there.

Developing your archetype of a business owner also involves educating yourself about business, especially how to own a business. Of course you want to keep up with the professional development demands of your industry, but I find that a lot of business owners focus on their industry while ignoring, to their detriment, the need to learn skills as a business owner. Owning a business is a career in its own right. I am usually reading at least several business books at a given time, and I'm also regularly taking classes on various business topics. I know the more I educate myself on owning a business, the better I'll be at getting more business. And all of that training also goes into my business owner archetype, helping to create a more knowledgeable version of myself that I can draw on as needed for business situations.

Your archetype is the compilation of qualities and education, as well as who inspires you. I activate my archetype every time I put on business clothes, which help me to embody this version of myself. The business clothes are a signal that I need to become myself as a business owner. When I put the clothes on my personality changes to fit that archetype. You could do something similar. If you have specific clothes that you associate with your business, then when you put them on think of yourself becoming the business archetype. The clothes are your ritual outfit used to help you embody the identity of yourself as a business owner.

You could also associate the archetype with business actions that you need to. For example, if you own a brick and mortar business, you might use the activities you do in your business to activate and embody your business owner archetype. In my case, when I work on balancing the books for the business or I'm writing a blog about a business topic, I feel the business owner archetype come to the fore to keep me focused on business matters.

Discovering and Working with a Patron Spirit of Business and Other Business Entities

While the business plan is a good place to start with your

business, it is also essential to cultivate the right team for your business. Your team should be comprised of experts in their respective fields who can help you work on the aspects of your business that you are not an expert in. For example, while you do need to keep track of your business finances, you'll want to hire an accountant to do the business taxes, and if your business is big enough, you will likely need to hire an accountant to work full time at the business. An accountant is one example of a team member, but other examples include business coaches, business insurance, graphic designers, etc.

It is important to cultivate a business team because you will find that you don't want to do it all yourself. Outsourcing a lot of the work of running a business is a smart move because it allows you to focus on what is truly important, which is growing the business and providing your clients the best possible service. A business team provides you people that you can go to when you have problems, and additional resources that those people are attached to. And I can't stress this point enough: If you want your business to succeed you need to invest in it. You may be tempted, especially at the beginning, to do it all yourself, but you will burn out quickly. Outsourcing some of the work may cost some money, but it will also save you time and be less stressful than trying to do it all yourself.

However your business team shouldn't just be comprised of people. You should also work with a patron spirit of business. A patron spirit of business is a spirit that supports and protects your business and can be called upon to help you draw in more business (Mierzwicki 2008). It can even be helpful with business advice, though it's always important to remember that its perspective on your business won't necessarily be informed by the context of your life, so such advice should be considered in that context before following through on it. Likewise, if you call on your patron entity for help with your business, be very specific about what kind of help you'd like it to offer. For example, if you own a part time business, and work a full time job and you call on your patron business spirit to help you with your business, you need to specify that you don't want it to cause you to lose your job. While losing your job would free up more time to work on your business, it might also cause a lot of stress because you needed the resources your job provided

(Miller 2012).

You can work with one of the wealth deities mentioned previously, or you can work with one with which you are familiar. In your shop or office you should create a shrine for the deity where you will honor him/her each day. An offering should be made to the shrine regularly, as a way to thank the wealth deity for its blessings in your business. In my case, my shrine is dedicated to Bune. I have a painting of his sigil above the shrine and on the shrine I have various items associated with wealth including my business checkbook and any checks I've received from clients. One of my offerings is the writing I do about him, but he also wants any wealth artifacts to be placed on the shrine as both an offering to him and a way for him to charge them. Your deity may have different requirements for you, but you'll want to honor whatever agreement is developed.

As a patron spirit, Bune offers me advice on business strategy and actions. When he first started working with me, he told me that I needed to read more books on business development. He also told me that I should get out of the social media business I was in and do what I really wanted to do with my coaching practice. Finally, he suggested that I turn my magical experiments website into a business. I've followed his advice, and as a result I did move out of the social media business into business coaching and am much happier. I'm also seeing much quicker success. Reading the books on business development has helped me become better at running my business, while providing valuable tools to my clients. And turning Magical Experiments into a business and starting the Way of the Magician Mystery School has allowed me to take my experience as an author to a whole new level. Even now, Bune continues to provide advice and the advice is always spot on. In return, I continue to make my offerings to him. It is a business relationship that has proven to be beneficial to both of us.

Sometimes you may need to create or bring in another type of entity that focuses on a specific area of business. In January of 2013 I was feeling really frustrated with my sales. I couldn't seem to close any sales, and no matter what I did magically or mundanely none of it seemed to take. I decided to create a magical entity that would help me improve my sales. I created a painting that I used as its housing and initially fed it with my feels of stress and frustration, but also made part of its fuel source the actual sales process. I wanted it to help me improve my sales, so it needed it to be fed by the sales process so that it would be motivated to find more opportunities for me.

Right from the beginning I saw results. I was suddenly booked to do special guest speaking opportunities for a networking organization I belonged to. At those meetings I was able to make a special offer that would allow people to work with me for an hour of coaching while paying me a reduced rate, and I had some takers. Nonetheless, I still wasn't closing sales the way I hoped I would be. I posted about the issue on my blog and one reader suggested that I link the entity to what I was reading about sales so that it could help me. I hadn't thought to do that initially, so I gave it a try and shortly after doing this I closed my next two sales calls. Not only that, but I also felt much more comfortable in the sales calls because I felt like I had an adviser on hand who could walk me through the process.

As you can see, creating or working with an entity doesn't automatically solve your problem, but it can still be helpful. Even from the beginning the sales entity worked, but I needed to refine it further to get the results that I wanted to achieve. And that couldn't have occurred if I hadn't gotten some advice from someone else, which just shows how important it is to bring issues to your network. By refining the entity I improved it, and in turn it's helped me get the results I wanted to achieve. Now when I go to a sales call I feel that it is nearby, ready to offer advice and help me draw on the sales knowledge I've read, as well as offer insights about the person I'm meeting with.

Your business problem may not be sales. It could be marketing, finances, work-life balance or something else. You can create an entity for each of those specific areas with the purpose of the entity being to help you improve your skills in that area. Just make sure you link the entity to what you are reading and doing so that it can take in what you are doing and then offer suggestions and skill enhancements that will help you improve those areas of your business.

Conclusion

Owning a business is a lot of work. Employing strategic

resources, both mundane and magical, can be helpful for making the work easier. If you need any additional help, I recommend looking into resources such as SCORE or the Small Business Development Center (SBDC) or hiring a business coach such as myself to help you work through the issues that are holding your business back. You can contact me for business advice through imagineyourreality.com

Chapter 8: Wealth and Health

With the exception of one book on wealth magic, the majority of books on this topic focus on finances, job hunting and advancement, and in some cases, business magic. Jason Miller's Financial Sorcery, the sole exception, touches on health, but mainly in context to changing financial habits. In this book I've taken a holistic approach to wealth, which means that while the financial aspects of wealth are an important part of wealth, it's equally important to focus on other elements of wealth, such as your health.

I see health as integral element of wealth because how healthy or unhealthy you are shapes the experiences of your life and your ability to enjoy and use your wealth in its financial form. There are different types of health. There is the physical health of your body, and there is mental health of your mind. Both forms of health need to be carefully cultivated, but doing this requires discipline and a clear understanding of what your health means to you as well as how it relates to your approach to wealth.

Health is tied into wealth, because how healthy you are plays a role in your ability to create wealth. If you are sick, disabled, or suffering psychological trauma, it can have quite an effect on your ability to acquire others form of wealth. However, even if you are healthy overall, your lifestyle choices can also impact your experience with other facets of wealth. Taking care of your health is important because of how it is tied into your ability to acquire wealth. Without health, it is much harder to get wealth, and indeed even to enjoy it, and to have health, you have to take care of yourself. Taking care of yourself means eating the right kind of food, getting the right kind and amount of exercise, and getting the necessary professional help needed to keep your mental and physical health in a good place. However even that statement doesn't fully convey what health really is or how we can cultivate it. So let's explore each facet of health in more depth and also look at where magic can come into the picture.

Physical Health: the image and the Reality

We are saturated with images of what a healthy person looks like every day. Actually what we are really exposed to are images of what a beautiful person looks like each day. However, beauty is not automatically indicative of health, and if anything, it is actually a standard of unhealthiness.

It's very important that you don't mistake physical health for image. In other words, don't get fixated on media images of what a healthy person looks like. A skinny person isn't automatically healthier than someone who has more weight. The goal of being healthy isn't to aspire to a specific image of what healthy looks like, but rather it is to develop a better relationship with your body. When you focus on the image of what you think healthy looks like or mistake it for beauty, it can take you down the wrong road, to the point that you end up being unhealthy. For example, if you have an eating disorder, or know someone who does, it usually occurs because you are trying to look a certain way and you mistake the look for the reality of being healthy. When I was in my early twenties, I was anorexic. I would only eat one meal a day because I wanted to make myself look a certain way. However looking that way didn't make me feel good about myself. I felt weak and irritable. Eventually I started eating more and I felt better. I realized that starving to look a certain way wasn't healthy. Unfortunately many people buy into the appearance of health and beauty while sacrificing the actual experience of it.

The actual experience of health involves the recognition that being healthy is more important than appearing a particular way. Being healthy means that you eat proper portions of food on a consistent basis and that you get the right kind of exercise to keep you in shape, and most importantly that you learn to accept your body as it is, instead of trying to make it into something it can't be. You may find that you are born with a body type that doesn't fit the conventional standard of health and beauty. No matter what you do, you can't change that, and you shouldn't. However what you can do is take good care of your body.

Part of the wealth work you need to do with your body involves examining your beliefs about your appearance and asking where those beliefs come from. I don't think you can really be healthy in your body until you've done the internal work around appearance and what it means to you. The obvious example of where your beliefs about appearance originate from is found in media, where we are bombarded with images of how mainstream culture thinks people should appear. This also occurs to a certain extent with subcultures. Certain images of beauty are typified and broadcast in subcultural media, and those become the standard by which people in the subculture can be judged. It's no surprise then that people's focus on health is defined in part by media.

But there are other factors as well. Friends and family can also play a role. When your mom or dad comment about how fat you are or how you need to lose weight, they also fixate on image. Rarely have I heard such a comment made out of concern for a person's health. And they also model their own issues around appearance, which can play a role in how we integrate appearance into health. Usually such a comment is made because of how a person looks. The same occurs with friends. We may feel like we are in a competition with friends or we might envy how they look. And sometimes friends will make comments as well about appearance which also have an impact on your self-image and how you relate it to your health.

There is also your significant other(s). S/he may also play a role in how you think of your appearance. When s/he comments about your appearance or compares you to someone else or just comments on what s/he finds attractive about someone or people in general can have an effect on how you approach your self-image, and how valued you feel by your partner. And if you ever had previous partners who cheated on you that can also affect your self-image as you question what they found lacking in you.

Your professional job is another factor in appearance. There are always expectations about how someone looks or should look. If a person is considered to be fat, s/he may not be treated with as much respect as someone who is skinnier. It's incredibly shallow, but so much emphasis is put on appearance that people obsess about it and how good they do or don't look. Women put on makeup, for example, because it is a societal expectation that is focused around appearance. And while men don't put on makeup, there is a lot of pressure about having a full head of hair versus being bald. I'm only touching the tip of the iceberg, but it should be apparent that expectations around appearance shape how we approach health, usually in a negative manner.

There are two final factors to consider about appearance and they are skin color and body type. Skin color is unfortunately also used to judge appearance, and even the shade of skin color can be used to judge appearance. For example in black communities, the lighter your skin color is, the better you are treated or placed, because light skin is considered a way to be more accepted (Alexander 2012). Skin color is used to justify a lot of standards of beauty and also how people treat each other. If you are white, for example, you will be treated differently than a black person will. You have privilege, because society, in a subtle (and sometimes not so subtle) way favors people who have lighter skin. If you are a white person, you are less likely to be pulled over or given a harsh sentence, compared to a black person who is more likely to get pulled over and get a harsh sentence (Alexander 2012). It is important to recognize that skin color is used to discriminate against people, and as such some people may dislike themselves because of their skin color. This is unfortunate, but the only way we can address this issue is to bring it up and discuss it, while also showing that skin color does not contribute to a person's beauty or intelligence, or anything else.

Body type is also a factor of appearance that people have limited control over. If you have a body type that causes you to have a large frame, there isn't anything you can do to change it. Some people are naturally skinny, some people are naturally obese, and some people are naturally in the middle. For example I have a medium body frame, so I'm in the middle. I'm not skinny, but I'm also not obese, at least in terms of my body frame. It took me a long time to accept my body frame, because I felt like I should be thin, but I know I will never be thin and I accept that, and also accept that I can still like my appearance.

Diet and exercise can help you control your weight to some degree but if you have a large frame, then your body needs to be larger. Unfortunately mainstream culture (and even subcultures) tend to glorify certain images of body appearance over others, without really considering that in some cases people have the body type they have and that is what they need to accept. Learning to accept your body type can help you when it comes to exercise and diet, because you'll know how to create a diet and exercise that fits your physical needs, and you won't have an unrealistic image of how you should appear.

Exercise

When you think about your body, or look at it in the mirror, what words or phrases come to mind? What emotions come up for you? Write down the words and emotions. Next, I want you to meditate on the words. Where did you first hear them? Who told you that word or phrase? How did it make you feel when that person said what s/he said.

Next I want you to revisit your emotions about your body. Are those emotions really your authentic feelings, or are they reactions to the phrases and words you heard?

My Struggle with My Body Appearance

When I was in my early 20's I was anorexic. I didn't want to gain weight or change from the way I had looked as a teenager. I wanted to stay thin, but my body wasn't staying thin. So I decided to only eat one meal a day. I was thin, but I was an unhealthy thin. You could see my ribs, my collar bones, and I didn't have a lot of energy. Eventually a girlfriend realized what I was doing and encouraged me to start eating. I felt better for eating, but I had to do a lot of work around how I felt about my body.

Years later, when my mom commented on how I had gained weight and looked fat, I realized that she had contributed to my perception that I needed to stay thin. She was always obsessed with her own weight and no matter how much weight she'd loss, she always felt she was fat. And she passed that onto me, both with her comments about my appearance and her own issues. When I recognized this, I was able to do some internal work which helped me get more comfortable with my body type and weight, though in the last year or so I have felt unhappy with how I've felt and appeared.

In October of 2012, I went in for a physical and discovered I weighed 255. I also discovered I was pre-diabetic. I was in shock, and I realized I needed to make some changes in my diet and exercising. I hadn't realized I was eating a lot of starchy vegetables, for example, such as peas and beans (I never realized they were so starchy!). Instead of trying to starve myself, I talked with Kat and we decided to get on the Nutrisystem diet. Additionally I started doing more cardio exercises. At the time of this writing I weigh 225 and I'm no longer pre-diabetic. I am still on the diet and I am exercising regularly, although I'll be getting off the diet soon. I am watching the portions of food that I'm eating and being more conscientious about how my body feels as I eat.

I have come to accept my body type and I like my appearance overall. I'm dieting mainly for health reasons, though I'll admit I would like to look a bit slimmer. However I no longer want to try and have a skinny body. Not only would I look ridiculous, but I don't think I'd feel good either. Learning to accept my body as it is, and to work with it so I can be healthier has helped me accept myself overall.

Physical Health: Your Diet

Your diet is an important factor in your physical health and wealth. Many Americans are considered obese, in large part due to the kind of diet we have access to, but also due to the advertising and consumerism focused around the appetite. Turn on the television or drive around town and you'll see lots of commercials advertising fast food and how eating the fast food will make you feel good. And fast food is only part of the problem. In general, the diet that Americans have access too is one that is high in starch and carbohydrates. Whether it is pasta, potatoes, or other starchy vegetables such as beans and peas, it can be very easy to pack on a lot of calories and a lot of weight. The portion sizes of an American meal are large. Go to any restaurant and your plate will be heaped with food, a lot of which you actually don't need to eat. There is also a cultural message that many Americans subscribe to: "don't leave the table until you've eaten all the food off your plate." Consequently many people are full, but keep eating because they need to "clean" their plate. A lot of us don't even know what full really feels like. Americans have learned to associate the bloated feeling of eating with actual fullness, but that bloated feeling is really telling you that you've eaten too much.

Cultural Values around Food or Having a Healthy Relationship with Food

I mentioned some of the cultural values about food that occur in the U.S. What are some of the values that you've learned about food? What are the portion sizes that you typically eat? How does your culture treat food? Do you need to "clean" your plate? Do you know when to stop eating?

On the other side of the equation are the diets. There are tons of diets available to people, all with advocates who claim that their type of diet will actually help. However, one of the problems with diets is that you can lose a lot of weight, and then get it back if you don't know how to sustain the weight you wanted to reach. The body also can have an adverse reaction to losing too much weight too fast, which prompts a person to gain some weight back.

What we need to do is come back to a healthy relationship with food. This involves learning several skills that can help you have a better relationship with your food and your body. One of those skills is learning what types of food to eat. In the U.S. a typical meal can include meat of some type or a carbohydrate such as pasta, potatoes, and some other type of starchy vegetable, and bread. Drinks usually are fruit juice (if you're a kid) or beer or wine (if you're an adult). This kind of diet is unhealthy and not only leads to a lot of weight gain, but can an also lead to diseases such as Diabetes 2.

A change in diet is in order, where we cut back on the starches and sugars while balancing the remainder with healthier food. Instead of having a potato and green beans with dinner, try having a salad and green beans. You still get some starch, but you don't get as much. And when you have lunch, don't get fries with your burger. Instead, get a salad. Cutting down on the starches alone will improve your health a lot.

The other skill that we need to learn is portion sizes. Learning to eat smaller portion sizes can be hard, because we are so used to eating larger meals, but if we smaller portions and also have healthy snacks in between meals, it actually is much better for our bodies and allows our metabolism to process what is eaten at a rate that keeps the weight down. Part of how you learn to eat smaller portion sizes involves actively being mindful while eating and asking yourself if you've had enough food to eat. Because we are so used to associating the feeling of fullness with a sense of feeling bloated, it can be hard, initially, to recognize when you've eaten enough. What I do is track the feeling of hunger. If I feel hunger, I feel a gnawing sensation, which is my stomach telling me it needs food. However, if as I eat, I feel that gnawing sensation start to go away, then I need to keep track of that sensation and stop eating once it is gone. That means I'm full. If I continue to eat after that feeling has gone away, I'm overfeeding myself and eventually I'll feel bloated (which is what we typically associate with being full). The problem with being bloated is that not all of the food gets digested properly (which causes health issues of its own).

Being mindfully aware of your appetite involves actively monitoring it. When you first try to limit your portion sizes, don't watch T.V., read a book, or play a game. Focus your attention on your stomach and what you are feeling. Also eat slowly. A lot of people will eat as fast as they can, because they feel starved. Consequently, they don't pay attention to what their body is trying to tell them. You can alleviate the feeling of hunger by having healthy snacks during the day between the major meals. Each time you eat, slow down and really taste the food. Don't be in a rush to finish. By eating slowly you'll give yourself time to determine if you aren't hungry any longer.

It's also important to give yourself permission to stop eating if you haven't finished everything on your plate. You can always save the food for later, and if you can't do that, then compost it. The point is you shouldn't force yourself to eat more food than you need. Giving yourself permission to stop eating, even if there is food still on your plate, is healthy and sensible.

You might notice that I haven't included any magical actions you could take on the diet. The fact is that I don't think it wise to try and use magic to get yourself to diet. Or rather I think if you are going to use magic you need to do it in a way that works with your body as opposed to trying to force it to lose weight via magic. I feel that by working on the types of food you eat, as well as the portions, you can do a lot to change your weight, especially if you apply mindful awareness to your actions. With that said, the only magical work I'd recommend involves working with the consciousness of your body.

Exercise: What Are Your Cultural Values Around Food?

To work with the consciousness of your body, you need to travel into your body. The meditation I typically do for this purpose involves directing your consciousness into your body and travelling to the specific parts of your body that you want to communicate with. In the case of dieting, there are a few places that come to mind: your stomach (large and small intestines), your kidneys, your liver, and your muscles.

Your stomach contains all the bacteria that is used to digest food. Connecting with both intestines can help you learn how you are helping or hurting your stomach. You may even want to connect with the bacteria to learn more about them and what foods they feel is best for you. Your kidneys process your food as it turns into waste, and can give you some insights into your waste processes. Your liver also processes waste and should be connected with in conjunction with your kidneys. You'll also want to connect with your muscles to learn what kind of exercise they think you need to do, as well as to help you shape your body while dieting and exercising.

I want to offer one final tip about dieting. If you are on a diet, it's important to give yourself an occasional break from the diet. While I was on the Nutrisystem diet, I gave myself a meal or two a week that wasn't strictly on the diet. This made it easier for me to stay on the diet, because it was a reward for sticking on the diet overall, as well as continuing to exercise on a regular basis. It helped me keep my morale up and it gave me something look forward to each week I was on the diet.

Exercise: Traveling into the Body

For this exercise, I recommend lying down or sitting while you do this journey. You want to achieve a state of meditation, which you will then use to journey into your body. The meditation I typically do involves counting to 100 and relaxing your body. 1-10 relaxes your feet, 11-20 relaxes your calves, 21-30 relaxes your thighs, 31-40 relaxes your hands, 41-50 relaxes your forearms, 51-60 relaxes your shoulders, 61-70 relaxes your stomach and chest, 71-80 relaxes your neck, while 81-90 relaxes your heads, and 91-100 deepens the entire state of relaxation. When I do this meditation I will say something such as: "As I count from 1-10 I will feel a relaxing, tingling energy relax all the muscles in my feet."

When you've counted to 100, you'll visualize a door and the door will lead you into your body. You will feel your consciousness enter into your body and become a blood cell. You can use the blood cell to travel to your stomach, liver, or kidneys. Once you've encountered an organ you might ask it what advice it has for you, in terms of taking care of your body. Also if you journey to your stomach you might seek connection with the bacteria and get their advice. You can ask your organs and bacteria to appear before you and ask them for a symbol that you can use to contact them. This symbol will make it easier for you to connect with them in future meditations, as well as do work with those areas of your body.

If you visit magicalexperiments.com/wealthmagic I have a free MP3 available, which is a recording of the meditation.

Physical Health and Wealth: Exercise

While changing your diet is part of your health and the wealth it provides you, exercise is another essential element of your health. Exercising on a consistent basis is important for keeping yourself healthy. Ideally you are exercising every day or at least five days out of the week. You should exercise at least 45 minutes to one hour each day, in order to keep yourself healthy. You should also do your best to keep your weight down. The right exercise and food can help with that. However not just any exercise will do.

The right types of exercise are important, and the right types can vary from person to person. However there are still certain consistent standards that need to be applied. For example, you need to do some kind of cardio activity that gets your heart pumping for an extended period of time. You might also need to do some kind of resistance training in order to build your muscles up. At the same time the exercise you do should be something you enjoy doing, while also using it to improve your health.

I started doing Tai Bo again when I got on my diet and focused on losing weight. Tai Bo is a cardio/strength training form of exercise. I like to do it because it exercises all the parts of your body. Before that I had been doing pushups and sit-ups as well as going for walks, but the combination of those exercises wasn't providing me the needed amount of cardio-vascular stimulation or helping me to keep the weight off. I switched to Tai Bo because I realized I needed a system of exercise that would raise my heart rate, while also helping me exercise my entire body. Tai Bo works for me, but it might not necessarily fit you. Whatever does work for you does need to get you to exercise for an extended period of time. Going for a walk probably won't cut it unless you are doing speed walking and are really pushing yourself.

At the same time, the type of exercise also needs to fit what you desire for your body. I haven't done any strength training, beyond what I'm doing in the Tai Bo course, because I don't want to bulk up my muscle mass. If you want to bulk up your muscle mass, you may want to do some strength training or resistance exercises.

Staying on track with your exercising can be hard, unless you have the right motivation or motivator. In my case, I have found Tae Bo useful in part because of the instructor Billy Blanks. I treat him as a pop culture entity of exercise that calls me on my laziness, while also encouraging me to continue exercising. One magician I know used the Sergeant from Full Metal Jacket as his pop culture entity of exercise. If you have an exercise video you like to use, you can work with the pop culture persona of the instructor. If you don't have that option available, you might create an entity that helps you to stay on track. Spend some time thinking about what the entity will look like and how it will inspire you to stay in shape. You might feed it with the actual energy you put into the exercising, so that it is motivated to keep you in shape.

Taking care of your physical health is a cultivation of your wealth. When you are eating properly and exercising regularly you feel good about yourself, enjoy the world, and even have a way to work off some stress. However physical health is only one component of wealth as it is manifested through your body.

Mental Health and Wealth

Your mental health is just as important as your physical health when it comes to experiencing wealth in your life. Your mental health is affected by stress and trauma, as well as joy and bliss. Dysfunctional issues are symptoms of mental health, but they don't define mental health. What defines mental health and wealth is how well a person copes with the stresses of life, while also living the joy and bliss.

At the beginning of this book I discussed positive thinking at some length. Positive thinking is a form of mental wealth when used correctly. It is used correctly when it inspires a person to take action and find opportunity. When positive thinking is used incorrectly, it becomes a dysfunction, such as is found in the Law of Attraction. The Law of Attraction argues that by simply thinking of what you deserve you'll attract it, but its fuzzy thinking at best, and at worst leads people to believe that they must have attracted the circumstances they are in, without providing them a way to find opportunity in those circumstances.

To some extent all of the behaviors and emotions that we experience have both healthy and unhealthy expressions. For example, anxiety can be a healthy feeling to experience when a person is undergoing stress from a traumatic experience or is in an experience of survival, such as a fight or a hunt. Anxiety, in those contexts, is an expression or venting of the stress. However anxiety can also be a dysfunction, such as when a person allows it to rule every experience s/he has, or uses it to justify retreating from the world.

Anger is another example. It can be healthy when we express anger about a situation, but it can become unhealthy when we hold onto the anger or use it to justify behavior that is abusive. Recognizing the difference between healthy and unhealthy expressions of emotions and other behavior is important because it also helps us understand the mental wealth we have at our disposal.

Exercise

I want you to think about your most recent stressful experience. What emotions and behaviors came out? How did you express them? Do you feel your expressions were healthy or unhealthy and why?

Next think about the experience of being in love. How is this experience healthy or unhealthy? Can it be both and how do you determine when it is or isn't healthy?

You can take these exercises and apply them to any experience. What you will discover is that each emotion and behavior has a healthy and unhealthy component to it. When an emotion is experienced as an extreme or even as a lack of the emotion it can be unhealthy. However it can be healthy, when it allows us to cope with stress and experience joy in a meaningful way that still leaves us in a place where we can fully live life.

As you consider mental health/wealth and where it fits into your life, it's worth considering what the relationship of happiness is to mental wealth. In the U.S. there is an obsession with being happy. Everyone is supposed to be happy, and if they aren't happy, they aren't supposed to admit that they aren't happy. Consequently there is an obsession with being happy that ironically seems to make more people unhappy than happy.

Happiness is not indicative of mental health in my opinion. You can be mentally unhealthy and still feel happy. Happiness is just one emotion among many, and while it can be a wonderful emotion to feel, those who see to truly be wealthy in all ways recognize that each emotion has its time and place and that what makes someone truly mentally healthy and wealthy is learning how to be present with your emotions and using them to help you navigate the problems that come your way as well as celebrate the triumphs of your being.

In order to cultivate mental wealth we need to learn how to be in balance with what we feel. This means we need to learn how to accept what we feel instead of trying so hard to be in a particular state of emotion. If you genuinely feel happy, enjoy it, but if you don't feel happy, then allow yourself to feel that emotion and be present with it. If you try to repress it you will just be denying an authentic expression of yourself. By learning to accept our emotional states and work with them, we can learn how to be more present in our lives, and with our partner(s), family, and friends.

I recently realized that I had an unhealthy reaction to depression. I spent a significant amount of my childhood, teenage years, and early twenties being depressed. When other people feel depressed I have reacted in a way that has been less than supportive, because of having spent so much time depressed. My realization about depression and my reaction has helped me become more present with people who are feeling depressed instead of avoiding them and what they feel, but it only occurred when I spent some thinking about my own experiences with depression and recognized that I'd developed an unhealthy reaction to it.

Look at all of your emotions and ask yourself how you feel about them, and how present you are with yourself or other people when you feel them. Your awareness around your emotions will help you develop a more balanced relationship with them, which in turn will lead to mental health because you will be able to acknowledge and work with them more consciously instead of being ruled by them or avoiding them.

Spiritual Health and Wealth

Your spiritual health/wealth is the final component to be considered. As a magician, I find that spirituality plays an integral role in both my health and wealth. Spirituality provides an explanation and perspective of the world, as well as a way to ask questions and find answers. It also provides the magician a way to cultivate his/her internal resources, while creating relationships with external forces (though atheist magicians might argue it's all in your head). Being spiritually healthy involves the recognition that spirituality can enhance the health of a person, by being a source of comfort and empowerment in both good and bad times. Spirituality provides another angle to explore the world, as well as express your relationship to it, and whatever powers you feel are present within it. The right spiritual expressions ideally lead you to a place of spiritual health and wealth because they enrich your life and help you work through whatever is holding you back from achieving the reality you want to live in.

One of the benefits of magic is that it provides the magician a set of tools and techniques to resolve problems while also continuing to develop him/herself. Religions such as Christianity or Islam rely on a higher power and place the spiritual power in that higher power's hands. While the magician can work with entities, s/he also recognizes that s/he is ultimately responsible for the experiences that s/he has on this mortal coil, and on any other plane of existence. Magic is one of the means that s/he empowers and takes charge of his/her own spiritual health, instead of relying upon a deity.

Daily Meditation

One of the ways to cultivate spiritual health/wealth is to engage in a meditation practice on a daily basis. I know some people shudder at the idea of doing a daily practice, but in my opinion, if you are serious about magical work of any kind, you need to be doing daily work to cultivate your spiritual and mental resources. Much like with exercise, if you don't do it every day (or nearly so) you are allowing your muscles (mental and spiritual) to atrophy. Aside from that meditation enhances your creativity, while also grounding you emotionally. The rare days I don't meditate, I don't feel as grounded, and tend to be more scattered emotionally and mentally. Meditation also helps you relax and process stress, which is good for the physical health of your body.

As for what kind of meditation practice you do…it can be a Western or Eastern magical practice, or a combination of both. I have found the Eastern meditation techniques tend to focus more on internal work and dissolving emotional and mental blocks, while Western techniques focus more on visualization and connecting with powers around you. I think doing a combination of both is useful because it teaches you how to work with your own energy while also connecting with the world around you.

Regardless of what meditation practice you do, make it a part of your day, and if possible, do it during the same time of day. Your consistency will pay off not only in the enhancement of your physical and mental health, but also in terms of focusing your magical resources towards any spiritual or practical work you need to do. The more you make magic part of your life, the more easily you can apply it to achieve the results you need and want to enhance and enrich your life!

There are p!enty of books available on meditation, but my meditation practices of choice tends to be a combination of Taoist Breathing meditation and Dzogchen dream and meditation practices. These work for me because they allow me to cultivate my internal resources. However you may find Western practices better suited to you. Before I discovered the Taoist and Tibetan practices, I regularly did the LBRP, and several other Kabbalistic practices where you vibrated the different names of God. I stepped away from doing those practices because they were focused on cultivating a relationship with an external source of energy, as opposed to cultivating my own internal sources. Whatever your choices are they should be practices that you do regularly in order to strengthen your connection with magic, as well as enhancing your skills.

Magical Practice

I think that along with doing daily meditation, it's also good to be doing some kind of magical working on a regular basis. It can be a practical working, one for spiritual evolution, or a combination of the two. The reason for doing this is similar to why you do daily meditation. It's exercising your spiritual muscles, and it's also cultivating that spiritual wealth and health.

I am usually doing a least couple of ongoing spiritual workings throughout the year. I do my elemental balancing work throughout the year, and then I have other projects I work. Of late, I've been doing a lot of work with dreams, but also with practical wealth magic. I'm also doing some Qabalistic work with my wife. Doing magical work on a regular basis keeps you sharp and also helps you find opportunities, which is important for the wealth work that a person does.

Your magical work should be different from your daily meditations. They should be major undertakings that you are involved in, with specific goals in mind. Ideally your magical work isn't done as a reaction to a situation, though sometimes that is what prompts the need to do magical work. However, if that is the case more often than not, it would be a good idea to do some internal work and figure out how you are participating in situations that call on you to use magic reactively. The majority of magical work I do is proactive, designed to head problems off or provide me necessary skills I need to improve what I'm doing and how I'm doing it. By approaching your magical practice in a similar way, you can employ it to produce more wealth of all types in your life.

Conclusion

Your physical and mental health is part of your wealth. Without either you can't enjoy the material wealth you acquire. Additionally simply having good health makes life more enjoyable and enables you to handle challenges that come your way much more easily. I also think that when you examine physical and mental health as an aspect of wealth, it helps you appreciate how finite your life is and causes you to value it more. Time is perhaps the most obvious example. All of us only have so much time, but if we take care of ourselves physically and mentally, we can live longer lives, and enjoy more experiences. How we take care of ourselves speaks not only to our health, but also our capacity for wealth. A person who is mindful of his/her body and mind is someone who recognizes that life isn't boundless, and that the true enjoyment of life is discovered through actively enhancing the quality of your experiences.

Chapter Nine: Wealth and Relationships

The final aspect of wealth I am going to cover is relationships. When I use this word in context to wealth I'm referring to several different kinds of relationships, specifically professional connections, friendships, and romantic relationships. These types of relationships are an important part of your wealth. Indeed, I'd argue that you can't be wealthy if you don't have meaningful relationships in your life, because part of what makes a person wealthy is the ability to share that wealth in meaningful ways with the important people in your life.

A relationship of either type takes some work to develop and maintain. This chapter will only touch on some of the work that needs to be done to make a relationship of either type successful, but it is my hope that it will also help you recognize the connection between wealth and relationships. I have to be honest and admit that I've only come to understand this connection myself within the last few years. Before that I took my relationships for granted, in large part because I was used to only having a situational connection to the people in my life. In other words, the situation defined the relationship more than the actual connection did.

A situational relationship is a relationship where the situation defines the relationship and whatever potential the relationship has. I don't think I'm the only person who has ever approached relationships as situational, but the problem with such an approach is that a person is only motivated to invest in the relationship when the investment applies to the situation instead of investing in the relationship in and of itself. Because the relationship is defined by the situation, the situation puts limiting parameters into place that make it hard for people to genuinely engage each other because they know that the situation dictates what the relationship can be. Instead the relationship should define the situation.

A situational approach to relationships is a transactional relationship, as well as one based on survival. What this means is that the relationship only exists as long as the situation is unchanged, and when the situation changes, the relationship is evaluated, to determine if it is still of value. As you can probably tell such an approach to a relationship is rather mechanistic, looking to the parameters to define the value of the relationship instead of looking at the value of the people. The reason such relationships are so prevalent in Western cultures is because they have been imbedded in our culture. We have only to look at the concept of a dowry, where the bride's family pays the groom's family to "buy" the daughter to see this in action. Arranged marriages are another symptom of this thinking, and although we might like to think we've progressed from such a transactional model, it is still very much in place in modern society.

We see the transactional aspects of relationships in a variety of relationships. Your job is a transactional relationship predicated on the exchange of service for income...if you own a business the transaction is based on your expertise. When you are a friend to someone or a lover, a transaction is more subtle, but is still present in how you treat the person, and what you are willing to do. Perhaps that sounds cynical, but Western capitalistic culture glorifies transactions and presents them to us all the time. Acknowledging this aspect to relationships can help us determine if we are focused more on the transactions or more on the actual relationship. If we are focused on the transactions then we are letting them and the situation they occur in define the value and importance of the relationship. This approach to relationships is one based on scarcity, because the focus is on how you can get value from the relationship and what the relationship provides you, as opposed to being in a genuine relationship with the person.

My Experience with Situational Relationships

Most of my relationships have been situational relationships. I learned early on how to appraise people and determine whether they were of value to me or not. This was a valuable survival skill, because I wasn't popular, and I also had a bad home life. I learned that appraising the value of a relationship could help me determine how best to use that relationship for my benefit. In short, I was manipulative. I learned how to use other people and any relationship I had, friendship or otherwise, was based in part on how valuable someone was. I also learned that other people would use me the same way. For example, my father leveraged me against my mother while he had custody of me, and later on she did the same when she had custody. The various "friends" I had were similar. We learned how best to use each other to get what we could from the relationship.

Even after I became an adult I approached each relationship as situational, which is likely why I don't have many friends from the old days. Once I left a situation, I let go because the relationship no longer had direct bearing on my life (as far as I knew). I have always been a loner, and I had an expectation that people really only wanted to be in my life because of what they could get from me. I've seen this borne many times over in my life, but I also recognize that I've contributed to this particular perspective of relationships. Over the last few years my view on relationships has changed, and as a result I have actually formed some genuine relationships as well as managed to continue a few that had been in my life even when I had a situational perspective.

As you can see, a situational approach to relationships is not a wealth approach to relationships. It is a survival approach, based on a belief that people will use you so you may as well use them, and also based on a belief that any relationship has a finite value and once that value is transacted or used up, the relationship no longer matters. This approach to relationships leaves a person with few friends and a lonely life.

There's one other thing I'd note about this approach to relationships. When you approach relationships in this way, it is hard to be genuine with other people. You learn how to appraise people and you learn how to study behavior so that you can demonstrate specific behaviors, but you don't really feel those emotions and the behaviors aren't genuine. How can they be, when you don't know how to connect with a person and only value him/her for what s/he can provide?

What is a Wealth Relationship?

If a wealth relationship isn't situational, the natural question to ask is what is a wealth relationship? A wealth relationship is a relationship where the relationship with the person is valued over what you can get from the person. Instead of doing something for the person because you want to get something from that person, you do it because you genuinely want to help the person and appreciate him/her. We might even call this relationship an unconditional relationship, because it is a relationship that isn't based on the situation or conditions within the situation. What defines the relationship is a genuine desire to connect with someone and be in that person's life regardless of what the situation is.

Unconditional love is usually associated with a wealth relationship. Unconditional love is the acceptance of a person as s/he is, but also an acceptance of the relationship as being of value regardless of the situation. However, unconditional love is not an unconditional acceptance of the person's behaviors. You can love someone unconditionally and disagree with them or have issues with how they behave. Unconditional love is not an invitation to walk all over someone, but it is an opportunity to love someone for who s/he is, as opposed to what s/he can do for you.

In fact, I'd argue that a wealth approach to relationships is actually a much better relationship in terms of boundaries than a situational one is. While a situational relationship is based on specific conditions those conditions aren't boundaries so much as they are specific determinants of whether the relationship still has value. In a wealth/unconditional relationship, the relationship always has value, but boundaries are set to ensure that each person feels valued as a person, as opposed to what s/he can do. The setting of boundaries is really the establishment of each person valuing their own sense of personhood enough to tell someone else that they need to be respected, and also in turn signal their own willingness to respect the other person.

Respect is another quality of wealth relationships. In a wealth relationship each person respects him/herself as well as the other person and the relationship itself. If there is no respect, then you are looking at a situational relationship, where the people are more concerned with what they can get, as opposed to how they can honor themselves and their partners. Being able to establish boundaries is one sign of respect, but another sign is being able to value the other person and being able to communicate work through issues together. When you respect yourself, you will naturally communicate with someone else you are in a relationship with because you will want to be respected by that person. That respect can't occur without good communication.

Communication is also a quality of wealth relationships. However, everyone communicates to one degree or another. So it's not so much communication as it is an ability to have a genuine dialogue with another person. A dialogue is a respectful interaction where each person listens to the other and yet both also feel they can say their piece. When we are in dialogue with another person, we are able to hold space with that person and really listen to what s/he has to say. We may feel reactions come up, but we are able to acknowledge and dismiss without letting them control our actions. Instead, the desire is to have a fully conscious interaction which allows both people to get to the root of any issue and work through it successfully.

I don't think many people have wealth relationships with their friends, romantic partners, or family. The reason I suspect is because the majority of relationships I've observed or taken part in have been situational relationships, with each person more focused on what they can get than what they can give. Nonetheless I do think it is possible to have a wealth relationship with your friends, family, and romantic partner, provided everyone involved is willing to work toward such a relationship.

Exercise

I want you to look at your relationships, both past and present. Would you characterize those relationships as situational or wealth relationships? What proof do you have that you were in one or another type of relationship? Why did the relationship end (if it did)? If your relationship hasn't ended, what do you think you can do to cultivate a wealth relationship? What qualities do you think are essential to developing a wealth relationship?

Finding the Right People: Part 1

In my opinion developing wealth relationships involves finding the right people in your life. Not just any person will do, and this is evident by the many dysfunctional relationships people get involved with. There is no such thing as a problem free relationship, but if you have consistently drama laden relationships then you need to look at both the relationships and your role in those relationships. While I covered what the difference is between a situational and wealth relationship, some further refinement is in order.

The word drama encapsulates a dysfunctional relationship. A person who brings a lot of drama into your life is someone who needs to be the center of attention, or is clingy and needy to a point where you feel drained by the person. S/he may also start a lot of conflicts with you or just be passive aggressive. You don't want drama in your life, but so many people have it in the form of unhealthy friendships and romantic relationships. Doing the exercise above can help you recognize if the relationship is a situational or wealth relationship, but you should also pay attention to how you feel around the person. Do you feel consistently drained by the person? Do you look forward to seeing the person, or do you feel like you are walking on eggshells whenever you are around the person? Do you spend most of your time fighting, or are you intimately connecting with the person? Do you feel like you can open up and genuine with the person or do feel you have to keep part of yourself closed off? Answering these questions can provide you some insights into whether or not the people you are spending time with are the right people for you. If you feel like you are always in the center of drama then one part of the problem is the people you are spending time with.

Even in a healthy relationship there will be times where you feel drained or there is conflict. This is a natural part of the life cycle of any relationship, but if you feel drained or are in conflict the majority of the time then the relationship isn't healthy. If you recognize that the relationship isn't healthy stop associating with the person. I recognize that may not be easy to do, but continuing to be in an unhealthy relationship will be much harder for you. As long as you participate in an unhealthy dynamic you will continue to allow yourself to be a victim of that dynamic. When I recognize someone is unhealthy for me, I stop associating with the person and I do a banishing ritual to remove the influence of the person from my life.

Banishing Rituals

For the banishing ritual you need a piece of paper, a pen, a lighter, and something to burn the paper in. Write the person's name down and then create a sigil from the name. You can create the sigil by getting rid of repeating letters and using what's left to create a symbol or just rearrange the letters of the person into a sigil. I've even taken the first letter of the first name and the first letter of the last name and combined them into a sigil.

Once the sigil is created, think of the person. In fact, let yourself feel the emotions you have about this person. Then allow yourself to "vomit" the thoughts and emotions onto the paper. Basically just feel the energy, thoughts, and emotions associated with that person come up your throat and then allow your mouth to open and let yourself gag for a moment so as to induce a vomiting like sensation. You will feel all the emotions, thoughts, etc. flow from you onto the paper. Then light the paper on fire and burn it to ashes. Take the ashes to the edge of your property and scatter them on the road, while telling the person to go out of your life.

This banishing ritual has helped me get rid of a few people. Right after I did the ritual the people stopped showing up in my life. I've also used this ritual to give me closure for people who haven't been in my life for a while, but nonetheless still had an emotional connection to me. By banishing the emotional connection I felt much better and no longer thought of those people.

There's another technique you can use that I first wrote about in Space/Time Magic. On a piece of paper draw a circle and place your sigil in the center of the paper. Draw other circles near the first circle and put into those circles sigils that represent people, events, place, your job, or anything else of importance to you. Draw a line to connect the central circle to the other circles. Now take up a pair of scissors and cut out any bubbles with sigils that you don't want in your life any longer. Take the cut out bubbles and burn them, or do what I did above with the first banishing ritual. I've used this technique to remove multiple unhealthy situations and people from my life and they've never come back into my life.

The point of doing a banishing ritual such this is that it helps you remove someone from your life, while also providing a sense of closure for you. Instead of continuing to hold on to the emotional baggage that the person has left you, you banish the person and banish any linger energetic and emotional connection to the person. This doesn't mean that you suddenly don't have to work through the issues that the person left behind, but rather that you recognize that you don't need the added complication of that person's emotional connection to you. By banishing the connection to the person you are letting go of the person and allowing yourself to start healing so that you can fully address those issues and learn from them.

Finding the Right People: Part 2

Getting rid of the wrong people, the ones who cause drama, is a good first step, but finding the right people for your life takes some work. When I talk about the right people, I am not talking about people who say yes to you all the time or agree with everything you say. I'm talking about people who genuinely like you for you, and if they disagree with you, they do so in a respectful manner. I'm talking about people who can say no to you because they respect themselves and you enough to actually care and not want you to walk all over them. But I'm also talking about people who have shared interests and want to spend time with you. They are people who will look out for you when you are ill, support you when life has kicked you down, and celebrate with you when you experience a triumph. These people are your friends and your lovers.

There's another type of right person as well and this kind of person is found in your network of acquaintances. S/he might be a co-worker or someone that you do business with, or a neighbor. These are people that you may not know that well, but they are useful to know because of who they know. I'm an avid networker and I can tell you that I know many people as acquaintances. The value of knowing them is that if I have a problem or someone I know has a problem, I can find someone who can solve that problem. By getting to know people around me, I've been able to learn who has access to what resources and how they can help me or someone I know. I've also been able to help those people connect with each other and with people in need of their services, by understanding what a given person does and then thinking about the people who need that person. There is real magic in having that kind of awareness of what other people do and how they can help you or someone around you.

I've even applied space/time magic to my network. I use my web of time and space on occasion to help me find someone. Even If I'm not currently connected to the person, at one time I was, and I can use the web to access that past connection and connect with the person. How I did this involved picturing the person in my mind, and then accessing the web of space and time to find the past connection. I can then interact with that past version to get some advice or suggestions, or even see if the past version can direct me to where the current version is.

There is a third kind of right person as well and this is someone who is a mentor. S/he is more successful than you are and inspires you to become more successful as well. S/he has advice to offer and will always push you to succeed. S/he sets the bar high and is someone you want to learn from because you know that it will help you achieve more success.

Finding the right people for your life doesn't have to be hard, and doesn't necessarily involve magic, though that can be helpful as well. Finding people who can be friends and potential romantic partners involves sharing what you like with people who like the same things. I met my ex-wife and my wife at pagan conventions, and I've met my friends through shared interests in magic, gaming, and books.

Finding professional acquaintances and mentors is also easy. If you work at a job find out what some of your co-workers are doing and if there is a person there that you respect a lot cultivate a relationship with that person by getting to know him/her and get his/her opinion on what you can do to become better at your job. If you are self-employed like I am, join professional organizations such as the chamber of commerce or industry specific organizations (this also applies to someone working at a job). Those organizations will provide you the opportunity to meet other professionals, who you can learn more about. Make a point to meet with your acquaintances one-on-one on occasion. This will both of you get to know each other better.

If you want to use magic to find people, the following workings may be helpful.

Passive Evocation

When I lived in Kent, Ohio I wanted to meet the local Pagan community. I had just moved there and I didn't know anyone. I decided that I'd create a passive evocation working. I took all the feelings, thoughts, etc. that I associate with meeting another pagan, and I evoked those experiences into Kent, Ohio. I did this an energetic working, so I evoked the feelings, experiences as energy that would point me to similar energy or the potential for similar energy. Whenever I felt an intuitive ping to go someplace or speak with somebody I followed up on it. The evocation was designed so that each time I made successful contact with someone who was Pagan, it would strengthen the evocation and help me discover more people.

You can take this working and apply it to your own search. Think about the kind of person or people you want to meet. What would the experience be like? What have past experiences been like? How did you feel? What did you enjoy about the experience? Once you feel that you've got the essence of the experience and feelings, visualize it turning into an energy (with a specific color, scent, etc. if needed) and then project that energy into the area that you live and send it out to find who you are looking for. I had results within a week, and you'll probably have a similar result.

How to Build a Community of Wealth with Your Friends

In previous chapters I discussed professional networking, but what about your friends? You've found the right people that are your friends, and so the next step is to build a community of wealth with your friends. A community of wealth is a community where you and your friends are spending time with each other regularly and enjoying the time you spend together. Your friends should enrich your life and you should enrich their lives.

Creating a community of wealth involves shared interests.

I mentioned above that you could find potential friends by going to places where you and the people there are doing activities of shared interest, but why not take it a bit further and make your own home a place of community activity? Kat and I host a Tuesday night board game night in our home, and once a month we do a magical experiments potluck. At each event friends come over and we enjoy their company, as they enjoy ours.

We'll also go to movies sometimes, to a board game day at the local game shop with friends, or go for a hike. Doing fun activities with your friends gives you opportunities to enjoy their company. Make a point to actually do those activities with them. And make a point to visit them and do activities in their homes as well. Get together for a dinner where the couples cook the meal together. Whatever you do, make it fun and make a point to do it regularly. When you enrich your life with the company of friends, you increase the feeling of wealth in your life, which is helpful in any wealth magic workings you are doing. Anytime I do a wealth magic working, I don't just use the feeling of getting a check from a client or getting a new client or even how I feel when I am taking care of a client. I use the feelings of networking, of friendship, of love and family and make that the nucleus of my working, so that I can inspire the wealth in my life for all the right reasons. After all I want any wealth that I bring in to be wealth I can share with the people who are most important to me. By drawing on how those people make me feel and infusing it into my wealth magic I am fully inspired to give my all to the magic so that in turn it can help me manifest more wealth into my life.

Speaking of relationships, the most important one is the relationship with your romantic partner. If you are looking for a romantic partner, the following evocation technique can be quite helpful in drawing him/her to you.

Evoking Your Romantic Partner

I've used this technique three times and each time it produced results, but I needed to tweak the technique each time because of characteristics I didn't factor in when doing the working. I urge you to only do this working if you feel that you cannot find a romantic partner in any other way, or if you are like me and have very specific ideas about what you want in a partner. Remember as well that there is a price for doing this kind of working in terms of how it connects you with the person and what expectations are built into the working. You aren't doing this working to get a one night stand, but rather to find someone that you'll ideally spend a lifetime with. As such it shouldn't be done lightly, but rather with recognition that you are doing a working to change your life in a very fundamental way.

Your first step (what I didn't do the first two times) is to define what you DON'T want in a romantic partner. You want to write down everything you don't want. If you don't want him/her to pick boogers out of his/her nose write that down. If you don't want him/her to be super clingy and needy for affection, write it down. If you don't want kids, write that down. Write everything down you don't want, but remember as well that you can still end up with someone who has a couple of attributes you didn't want. As long as they aren't deal breakers, keep yourself open to the possibility of the relationship.

Your second step is to write down what you DO want. Do you want someone who is monogamous or polyamorous? Do you want kids? Do you want someone who has an active sex drive or a lower sex drive? Do you want someone who can say no to you? Write down all the characteristics and details of the person you'd like to be involved with.

Your third step is to write about the relationship. What will this relationship look like? What kind of activities will you do with this person? What adventures will you go on? How will you handle conflict with this person? Take some time to really write down what you want your relationship to look like. If you don't like writing, you can also get creative with each of these steps and do some painting or another activity that allows you to represent what you do and don't want, as well how you want the relationship to look.

All of these steps should take some work. Don't share your results with anyone, because you'll have people tell you why what you want or don't want is wrong. They aren't you and they don't have to live with the result of the working, but you do, so keep it to yourself. Don't act on what you've written until you've given yourself a few days to think over what you wrote and you are sure that what you've listed is what you do and don't want in a perspective partner. The reason you do want to write or artistically represent these steps is because if you keep it all in your head, it's just a formless possibility. The very act of writing each of these steps is an act if manifestation. It starts the process of turning the possibility into a reality.

Your fourth step is to create a collage sigil. The collage sigil represents all of the information you put into the documents. Get some construction paper and some magazines, preferably ones that represent your interests. Start cutting out words and images that represent the relationship and the type of person you are interested in. Once you have cut enough words and images that you feel like you have enough to represent what you are looking for, put away the scissors and pull out the glue. Start gluing images and words to the paper in whatever order feels best to you. The words and images will represent what you are looking for in a relationship, while the glue will represent the process of attaching what you want to reality (which is embodied as the paper). Keep gluing words and images to the paper until you feel satisfied that the collage represents what you are looking for in a relationship. When you are done creating the sigil, you will have launched the evocation. The very acts of cutting and gluing serve as a creative channel of your energy that focuses your will into the collage, which in turn evokes the person into your life. Everything you want and don't want, as well as what the relationship will look like is also put into the collage by the act of creating it. The collage represents what you want and it will bring a romantic partner into your life within one year of its creation.

My History with This Technique

I developed the collage evocation in 2005. I've always liked collage as a creative and magical technique, and it can be very effective in terms of what it brings into your life. I have used this technique three times in my life, but the first two times I didn't write what I did and didn't want, or what the relationship would look like. Consequently there was a lot left to interpretation. The first collage brought my ex-wife into my life, while the second brought someone who ended up creating a lot of trouble in my life. The collages weren't created to help me find the perfect relationship (there's no such thing), but I realized that the more I left up to chance, the more variables appeared that effected the long term viability of the relationship.

The third time, as the cliché goes, is the charm. I defined what I didn't want in a romantic partner, what I did want, and what I wanted the relationship to look like. I found a partner within a few months that fit what I was looking for. She didn't have any anger issues, but could tell me no. She respected herself and insisted on being treated with respect. She was just as willing as me to work on the relationship and would be willing to stick with me for the long term. She had a similar background in magic and interest in experimentation. There were still a few variables, because I intentionally chose to keep myself open to the possibility of finding someone who fit the most important criteria, that didn't fit every detail I was looking for. I now have step kids, which I never planned for (but who have been really good for me, and I hope that I've been good for them as well). I am also now in a monogamous relationship, which has proven to be good for me because it's provided some good boundaries, as well as a concentrated focus on our happiness and the magical work we do together.

One point I wish to stress is that doing this work does not provide you a perfect relationship where there is never conflict. The truth is that any relationship takes a lot of work and dedication on the part of the people involved it (see below for some tips to that effect). This working may bring someone into your life, but you and s/he will still have to do work to make the relationship work. Accepting this important reality of relationships will help you make the most of the opportunity to be with someone who fits what you are looking for.

You might also decide at some point to destroy the collage. When I got a divorce from my ex-wife, one of the first actions I took involved destroying the collage I'd used to bring her into my life. I no longer wanted her in my life, and seeing it each day reminded of the connection to her. I realized that for me to have closure I needed to sever the connection, which involved destroying the collage. I ripped it up into little pieces and then burned it, along with the marriage certificate. I felt much better afterwards and the magical connection was severed. I still see her once in a while in a professional setting, but there is no connection beyond a brief period of time where we shared some history.

As I said before, be certain that you want to do this working. I chose to do it because I wanted to bring a magical partner into my life, but it took me three times to get it right. It also didn't help that I needed to work on certain relationship skills, but who doesn't? The fact is that while this magical working does indeed work, it will not solve all your relationship problems or automatically make you a better romantic partner.

Some Tips for Making Your Romantic Relationships Successful

Kat and I are going to write a book on the topic of relationships, but I want to leave you with some wealth tips for creating successful romantic relationships. Any type of relationship takes some effort, but in my opinion romantic relationships take the most effort. This makes sense because in a romantic relationship you are entwining so many levels of your life with someone else's, especially once you get to the point where you move in with him/her and share in the finances and daily living that occurs in such situations. The following tips are offered as guidelines to help you build and maintain a successful relationship. As someone who has admittedly had some unsuccessful relationships, I can safely say that if I had known these tips before I got into a relationship it could've saved me some grief or helped me recognize some red flags.

1. **When you initially fall in love, its neurochemistry and New Relationship Energy (NRE).** When you fall in love you tend to get stupid, in my experience. What I mean is that you are so busy feeling that wonderful neurochemical release of Dopamine (a pleasure neurotransmitter) and feeling the new relationship energy that you may not take as much notice of what bothers you about your romantic partner and whether what bothers is you something you can live with. NRE typically fades six months to a year into the relationship as your neurochemistry adjusts to the new person in your life. Thus when this occurs you may notice that certain behaviors irritate you more than they did before. My suggestion is take the first year of your

relationship and keep it slow. Don't rush into moving in with each other or getting married right away. Take your time and really get to know the person. If you still like and love him/her a couple years into the relationship and you both consistently make effort to make it work, then pursue a more serious commitment.

2. Sex isn't enough to make a relationship work. There is a lot of obsession with sex, but sex alone isn't enough to make a relationship work. While sex can be fun and be a very bonding activity, it can also cause a lot of stress. Don't make sex the central focus of your relationships, but instead recognize it as an activity that brings you mutual bliss with your partner. And make a point to just cuddle with your partner. Snuggling with someone you love can be much more bonding than sex sometimes and much more comforting when you really need it. I used to not be a snuggler, but I've since discovered that snuggling frequently has made me feel much happier and loved because it meets a primal need for affection and acceptance that sex alone won't provide.

3. Make sure you have enough interests in common. Just because you share one common interest with your partner, don't assume that alone will keep you together. In my first marriage my ex and I had similar interests in spirituality, but that was the only interest we had in common, and even with that interest, we ended up going in different directions. You want to be with someone who has multiple interests in common and wants to actively spend time with you pursuing those interests. For example, Kat and I both have a shared spirituality, a shared interest Science Fiction and Fantasy, a shared interest in board and video games, and we also like to go on adventures and travel. Those shared interests make the relationship much more fun and exciting.

4. Have proactive instead of reactive conversations. Relationships can be stressful because when you are with someone you get to not only experience the wonderful aspects, but also the annoying aspects. Additionally you and anyone you are with has past emotional baggage, and that baggage will play a role in your relationship. Instead of waiting to discover the baggage and have the inevitable reactions, I recommend having proactive conversations. The best way to do this is to pick up some books on relationships and read them together, one chapter at a time. When you've both read the chapter, sit down and talk about the chapter and what it brought up for each of you. Listen to each other and have a dialogue about the issues that were raised. By having a proactive conversation, you can defuse a lot of reactions and make other reactions much easier to handle because you will both know each other and will have a common dialogue about love and relationships. Another benefit of reading books on love together is that it creates intentional intimate time that allows you to get to know each other more deeply.

I recommend reading books on every aspect of love you can read about, which means reading books ranging from topics such as infidelity to what you do to keep a relationship passionate. You aren't reading the books to plan for the worse, but rather to learn about each other and discover the skeletons in each other's closets. I have a list of books on relationships listed in the bibliography. Reading these books has helped Kat and I have some very intimate conversations and greatly contributed to the wealth of our relationship. It's also helped me have some conversations with my friends and parents and allowed me to learn the family history around some of my core wounds.

5. Read books on finances, spirituality, and other interests together and discuss them. While reading books on relationships can be useful for creating proactive conversations, I also recommend that you read books on finances and spirituality. You may even want to read a science fiction or fantasy book together. Just as with tip four read a chapter at a time and then discuss what you read. In the case of finances, this will help you get on the same page as your partner and help you develop financial skills together. In the case of books on spirituality, you will be able to learn about what each of you believes, which can also be very rewarding. Kat and I read six books at a time together, which includes a book on relationships, one on finances and four on spirituality or on topics of interest that we both want to learn more about. At the time of this writing we are reading the New Jim Crow and learning more about critical race theory.

Even if you don't like to read much I do recommend reading a book on relationships, finances, and spirituality together. The conversations you will have a result will enrich your life and help you really get to know each other and yourselves.

6. Practice Magic together. Don't just talk about magic. Make it a point to do magic together. Kat and I meditate each night and we're currently working our way through a book on Qabalah, doing the exercises together. By practicing magic together we are learning more about each other and building a spiritual bond that allows us to help each other in our everyday lives.

7. Make sure you share the same sense of humor. You may think you are funny, but your sense of humor won't be for everyone. Just make sure the person you are with has a similar sense of humor. My ex-wife and I have very dissimilar senses of humor, so we found each other to be annoying and irritating. Kat and I, on the other hand, have very similar senses of humor. We are both silly, like fake accents and enjoy bursting into spontaneous song or just being weird for the hell of it. Having that shared sense of humor with my partner has greatly improved my happiness.

8. Be open and honest and claim your end of responsibility. Conflict is an inevitable reality of relationships. Kat and I sometimes argue. The key is to make sure that you are open and honest about how you feel, while also listening to your partner. And take responsibility for your end of the issue. It takes two to create a conflict, but neither person is entirely in the right. When you recognize this you can learn to take responsibility, which will help defuse the situation. And if either person shuts down, don't leave and don't continue the argument. Instead hold each other and hold space. In fact, I'd suggest that if you start to argue, take a few deep breaths and then come back and discuss it. If you are really upset, suggest that you want to take a walk and, when you come back you'll talk about it. By the time you are done walking you'll have cooled your temper down and you'll be able to talk about the problem more objectively. Any problem can be resolved with a steady mind and a willingness to listen as well as speak.

9. Go on holidays that are just for you. I used to be a workaholic and any trip I went on had to be a business trip. What a way to kill a relationship. Business trips can be fun, but for your relationship you need to go on trips that are just for you and your partner. If you have kids, a family trip can also be fun and is important for bonding as a family, but you still need to have trips that are just for the adults. Those trips will give you and your partner time to be with each other, explore a place, and most importantly will help you check-in with each other so that you can really be present and enjoy each other's company.

10. Make dedicated daily time for each other. When Kat comes home from work, I stop whatever I'm working on and we make time to connect. We hold each other and check in about each other's day. We eat dinner and talk some more or watch something we like. We make time for each other, because we recognize that if we don't the relationship won't last. Make time for your partner. Make your partner the most important part of your life. You'll always have work to do, and so it'll be there the next day. Your partner is more important and you and s/he will be happier if you make the effort to spend time with each other regularly.

The Wealth of Family

At some point you might decide you want to have kids with your partner. Or if you are like me, you may become a stepparent if your romantic partner has children. The following tips can be helpful when it comes to building and maintaining a family:

1. Your family is a responsibility you can't walk away from. Once you have kids in your life, they are there to stay. You have a responsibility to them, which means you need to be actively involved with their lives. Even in the case of a divorce you can walk away from the ex, but the kids are still part of your life and they need you to help them get through the messiness of the divorce. I wish I didn't have to write this tip, but the sad fact is many a parent does walk away from their responsibility to their kids.

2. Make time with each individual family member, as well as your family as a whole. Making individual time is important because you get to know each person of your family as a person. With your kids, it may mean showing interest in activities they are doing that they like, even if you could care less about them. What's important is that you consistently show up and show interest. Do activities with each member of your family. Also do activities as a whole. Go on a hike or a picnic together. The time you make to spend with your family will help all of you get closer to each other.

3. Take family vacations. Just as you need to take trips that are just for you and your lover, you also need to take family trips. Kat and I took the kids to Bend, OR for half a week. It was a good way for all of us to connect. We hiked, played Ping Pong and cooked meals together. Spending that time as a family, away from familiar surroundings got us out of our usual routines.

4. Know when to be strict, but also when to be fair. Kids need discipline in their lives, but you need to be fair. In my childhood, my father and my step-mother grounded me for the slightest infraction and even when I wasn't grounded would tell me what I could or couldn't do. It created a lot of resentment on my part, because they didn't know how to step away and let me develop. I needed discipline, but over doing it ultimately creates rebellion.

5. Do your best not to past your family baggage onto your kids. We all have emotional baggage, but one of the responsibilities of parents that have to their kids is to do their best not to pass their baggage onto their kids. That probably seems impossible to do, but I think if you are working on yourself regularly then you can recognize how your issues are showing up in the lives of your children and make some adjustments accordingly. At times, with my step kids, I've found myself wanting to be the harsh dictator that my parents were to me. I've always stopped myself and recognized that showing up in that way won't help me or them. When I feel that part of me come up, I will take some deep breaths and ask myself what it is I want to accomplish with them. Then I'll talk with Kat about it and we'll problem solve together before presenting it to the kids.

6. Teach your kids about finances early. Your kids can't learn about finances soon enough in my opinion. Finances will always be a part of their lives and you need to recognize that they will learn about finances the same way you did, based off observing how you handle your finances. If you're reading this book you've likely wanted to improve your financial situation. Do your kids a favor and pass that onto them. Talk with them about finances, not only generally, but also in specific situations. Kat and I are transparent about our financial situation with the kids. We work to teach them how to be more financially responsible by talking with them about how they spend and save money and helping them set up savings accounts where they can keep track of their money. At the same time we also let them make their own choices, but we'll discuss those choices to help them understand the consequences of whatever they choose to do financially.

Conclusion

Your relationships are part of the wealth of your life. Ask yourself this: Do my relationships lift me up or push me down? If they don't lift you up, they aren't relationships of wealth. A wealthy relationship is one that enriches and inspires both of you. In my opinion, you can't experience true wealth unless you have people in your life that make your life wealthier for their presence. Celebrate those people and your celebrate what makes life great, which is the shared community and love that is the most priceless evidence of wealth I've ever seen.

Conclusion

It is my hope that this book has given you some inspiration and direction in your own pursuit of wealth. I think that wealth magic is one of the more essential practices of magic, because in order to really pursue what you are called to do, you need to have a stable foundation. That stable foundation isn't merely a monetary foundation, but also one of health and love. As such I'd urge you to not just focus on the obvious form of wealth, but also examine how other aspects of your life are connected to what you define as wealth.

I've purposely chosen to write this book and show in the process of that writing my own journey to wealth, complete with my mistakes as well as my successes. I have some debt at the time of this writing, but far from feeling that this takes away from the legitimacy of this writing, I actually feel that it informs that journey toward wealth. Every person I know has been in debt, and if we are to truly achieve wealth we first need to be comfortable with the reality of being in debt, as well as learning how to move away from it. I wanted to show, as well, that you could get free of debt as I did and have circumstances occur that were out of your control that put you back into debt. I know I will be back out of debt, but I also know that under the right circumstances I could be back in as well, and knowing that there are tools, magical and mundane, to help me get back out and invest for the future is an essential skill for developing wealth.

What I have also discovered about wealth is that while it begins with responsible money management and investment, it doesn't end there. Your health and your connection with people are just as valid forms of wealth, and need to be cultivated just as you'd cultivate your money. We don't typically associate wealth and relationships with wealth, but this is because there is a disconnect in Western culture, which emphasizes the need to label and define everything into neat little boxes. However a holistic approach, such as I've used in this book is not only more realistic, but is also more needed. The recognition that wealth isn't confined to matters of finances can help us critically examine other areas of our lives so that we can begin a process of improvement that enriches us and brings forth true wealth, which is living a meaningful life with joy and wealth.

If there is one last lesson I can impart it is this: it is very important that you discover not only what brings you wealth, but also that you discover what it means to have enough. We live in a consumer society which constantly bombards us with the message that if we can buy this product or that service, maybe we'll finally be happy, but that simply doesn't work. Buying into the materialism of Western culture only leaves you feeling empty and unfulfilled. There is nothing out there that can fill in the void within you. In truth, only you can do that work and such work, in part, is defined by your ability to define wealth and know when to recognize that you have enough and don't need anything more. The rest of the work occurs through your choice to pursue a meaningful path that connects you to others around you as well as the universe at large. It is through those connections that you will discover the ultimate wealth, a life with connections, a life where you have pursued a meaningful existence and contributed to the well-being of not only yourself, but all existence.

Taylor Ellwood
Portland, OR
May 2013

Appendix 1: The Importance of Creating a Team of People and Resources

One of the recommendations I make to business owners is that they put together a team of people and resources that they can draw on to address any issues or problems in their lives. I think that people in general should have such a team and I'd recommend that you keep a contact list on your refrigerator or somewhere else that you can access it. So who/what should be on that list?

I'd recommend that you put the names and contact information for the following on your list:

Accountant
Electrician
Plumber
Heating/Air Conditioning
Carpet Cleaner
Health Insurance
Car/house insurance
Lawyer
Auto mechanic
Veterinarian
Doctor
Dentist
Hair Salon
Chiropractor
Acupuncturist
Naturopath
Landlord (if you have one)
Emergency Services.
Trash
Cleaning Service
Gardener
Computer Repair
Real Estate Agent
Mortgage services

Financial Adviser
Bank

You may or may not need all of these categories, but having the resources you do need in an easy to find place will make it easy for you to contact them if there is a problem. If you are a business owner you may wish to add a few more categories:

Bookkeeper
Web Designer
Business consultant
Merchant Services
Logo Apparel and Printer
Graphic Designer
Office Supplier
Mobile App Designer
Search Engine Optimization
Social Media Consultant

These lists may not be exhaustive, so if there are other resources you'd use, put those on the list too! What's important is that you have people and resources that you can contact when you need something, or if you want to refer someone to them.

Appendix 2: Two Wealth Entity Case Studies

I'm going to share two case studies of wealth entities. One example is of a successful wealth magic entity, and the other example is of one that wasn't successful. I'll discuss why one was successful and the other wasn't.

Health Entity Hakson

Hakson is a health entity that Kat and I created for a family member who was ill. In the spring of 2013 s/he began to experience migraines and bouts of dizziness, and, as we discovered later, s/he'd also lost a significant amount of peripheral vision. Naturally, we were concerned and took him/her to the doctor, but the doctor and specialists couldn't seem to find what the issue was, so we decided to create Hakson.

We created Hakson during the 4th of July. We chose that date to capitalize on the energy of the holiday and the celebration of the birth of the U.S. We bonded Hakson to a statue of a woman holding a baby, putting the sigil on the bottom of the statue. We also decided to integrate sex magic into the creation of the entity.

When the fireworks started, Kat and I had sex, and after she'd cum, we put the head of the statue (which had been purified and sterilized) into her vagina. I then used it to bring her to another climax, using her liquid as part of the awakening process for the entity.

Within a week we both noticed that our relative seemed to be getting better. S/je was less dizzy, more energetic, and back to normal. Over the next month or so his/her health steadily improved. The doctors couldn't determine what was wrong, but /she'd been going through a massive growth spurt and apparently that can cause some of the issues s/he encountered. Additionally, his/her family on his/her father's side has a history with migraines.

In the meantime, Hakson continues to work on keeping him/her healthy, and his/her dizziness has disappeared. S/he's back to being active and playing sports once again, as well being involved everything else s/he likes to do.

Why I believed s/he worked was that we got very specific about what we wanted and we also kept the magical work simple, creating an entity to do the healing and using sex magic to power up the entity and create sympathetic resonance between Hakson and Kelson.

Legal Entity Esacniw

Between 2011 and 2013 I'd gotten a total of four speeding tickets, which resulted in a suspended license for a month. One of the tickets had fallen off in March of 2013, but in June of 2013 I was pulled over by a cop for making an illegal change of lane. Even though it wasn't a speeding ticket, I once again faced the issue of not having a license for a month, as well as accompanying issues with the insurance.

I'm a member of Legal Shield, so I availed myself of their services and was assigned a lawyer. I also decided to work with an entity called Esacniw. David Michael Cunningham had created him for a trial of his own way back when and wrote about his success in *Creating Magical Entities*, so I figured he could be the entity to work with.

Right from the beginning there were problems. The lawyer I was assigned was a mediocre lawyer who did the bare minimum to help me with the issue, but perhaps the biggest problem was me and my inability to focus on one specific desired outcome. When I accessed Esacniw, I provided him multiple possible outcomes, but didn't consider that what I really needed to provide was one detailed outcome I wanted to manifest.

By not focusing on one specific outcome, I didn't adequately use Esacniw's talents to generate a specific desired outcome. By the time the trial occurred, I as nervous and unfocused and I couldn't sense Esacniw at all. I lost the case and paid the fine.

It occurs to me that one of the other issues is that I didn't create the entity, but instead used a pre-existing one. It may have been more useful for me to create one, especially as it would have helped focus my intention and efforts better than the pre-existing one did. That and the lack of focus on a specific outcome assured that the magic didn't work.

As an interesting aside, while I did end up paying for the fine, my license was never suspended (even though I had enough tickets at the time). I'm not sure why it didn't happen and I'm not inclined to assume that the entity was responsible. But I'm glad it didn't happen, as it would've been quite inconvenient. Since then I've taken to driving much more carefully and being very watchful for cops as well as the cameras they use to nab people driving.

Appendix 3: An Example of a Reactive Wealth Magic Working

Author's note: This article was originally publishing in Manifesting Prosperity. I've republished it here as an example of a reactive wealth magic working. My contemporary commentary is included at the end of this article.

How I used Wealth Magic to Move to Portland

In February 2007, I realized with complete certainty that I wanted to move to Portland, OR. My ex-wife Lupa and I had just finished vending and presenting at the Magickal Winter Weekend festival. What struck me most about that weekend was how active and supportive the community was, and how much I wanted to belong to a community like that. As we drove home to Seattle, a place I didn't like and felt little comfort in, I told Lupa how much I wanted to live in Portland and all the reasons why. At the time, she seemed to agree with me and I called some of my friends in Portland to tell them the good news.

A week later, Lupa brought up a point that had been bothering her all week long. She'd recently gotten her first tech writing contract. If we were to move at the end of the lease, it would be in April, but her contract wouldn't end until November. She didn't want to break her contract early, and told me she wanted to stay in Seattle until it was done. To say I wasn't happy would be an exaggeration. I suddenly felt as if I'd been offered the world and then had it taken away. When I posted my dilemma to a trusted list of friends the best answer I got was to either tough it out or consider moving down to Portland without her. Neither choice was viable and I was frustrated. Yet within a couple of weeks, by happy coincidence, Lupa was informed by her boss that her contract was ending early because he couldn't find time to train her.

Never one to look askance at opportunity I pointed out to her that I felt that the loss of her job was a sign from the powers that be that Portland was the way to go. After some thought,

Lupa agreed and we decided that we were Portland bound. The only question was how we were going to land what we needed, i.e. a job, a place to live, etc., in a manner that didn't hurt our finances. As I'd already been doing a lot of reading about finances and been working hard at changing my internal attitude to wealth, I was fairly certain I could come up with some viable magic that could land us in Portland safe and sound.

The First Step: Building up Energy for the Move

I did face a minor problem with our move to Portland. At the end of May, Lupa and I were scheduled to present at an event in Virginia and our tickets had already been paid for by the hosting event. The flight was scheduled to leave from SeaTac. I knew I could probably reorganize the trip to fly from PDX, but I also knew it would cost money. What this meant was that I had to time everything just right so that I moved down to Portland at the end of May instead of the end of April, when our lease was due to be finished.

I contacted our landlord and got her to agree to a one-month extension of our lease, if we needed it. Then I started job hunting. I put my resume up on all the main career boards and I started contacting recruiters for jobs. I also put a lot of energy work into the job hunt, using the Taoist technique of the macrocosmic circuit breath to accumulate energy and then direct that energy toward the job hunt. However, the energy work wasn't done to get a job right away. Instead it was driven toward making sure that everything fell properly into place exactly when we needed it and not one moment sooner. I didn't want a job in Portland until after our flight out of SeaTac had been taken care of, so although I started job hunting at the beginning of March I actually directed a lot of my magical efforts toward building the energy up and waiting for just the right moment to release that energy.

For many magicians, it seems that magic is results driven. Do some magic, get a result and move on with your life. I'm not really a results driven magician. I think results are important, but only in the sense that they confirm that your process is working or if it needs refining. To me, doing magic that requires a build-up and release is a process oriented approach. It doesn't focus on manifesting results right away and even when results manifest it doesn't stop with just those results. Instead the magician uses the results to build the process up, accumulating more and more energy, until eventually the energy can't be contained and it has to be released. The key is to release that energy in exactly the direction you want it to manifest.

The Second Step: Attracting Wealth and the Right Job

While doing the energy work, I also did several other magical workings that were designed to attract two important desires I wanted to manifest in Portland. The first important desire was to attract more wealth in my life. I reasoned that just by moving to Portland we could save money, but money alone wasn't what I wanted. Money is one external result or manifestation of wealth, but it doesn't comprise the entirety of what wealth can be.

To me the desire for wealth in Portland represented a variety of results I associated with being wealthy. Accumulating, saving, and using money wisely was one form of wealth I had already begun to manifest in my life, but wealth is more than just that. I still wanted to continue accumulating money, but I also wanted a less stressful commute, where I didn't have to drive nearly as much. I wanted to live in a really nice neighborhood, close to everything, but still have an affordable price on the actual housing. I also wanted to live close to the friends I knew, while having the opportunity to meet more people. I wanted to work magic with a group of people. Finally, I wanted to live in an area where I could continue to find and cultivate opportunities that would help me manifest one of my long-term desires, which is to become independent from working a nine to five job for someone else. All of these desires represented wealth to me and were fairly important in determining if Portland was the place to go.

The second important desire was to get a job at the right time. While it was true that I was already doing energy work, I also felt that having a little bit of help in finding a job couldn't hurt. I wanted to find the best possible opportunities so I could manifest them into my life.

I used two methods for working with these desires. The first method involved incorporating a statement of desire into my daily prayers. Each day I would pray to manifest the wealth of the universe into my life and also pray to manifest a job in Portland.

The second method involved creating two paintings. One painting represented wealth. I painted it to look like a magical dollar bill. I created the painting to act as a repository of wealth energy. The wealthier I got, the more wealth energy went to it, so that it could amplify that wealth energy into my life. The second painting was a painting used to create an entity that would help me find jobs. In the painting the entity stood above a jar with sigils. The jar with sigils stores away job hunting energy that the entity gathers. When I need that energy, I simply evoke the entity and have it release the job hunting energy. A nice extra feature is that even when I'm working at a job this entity can still gather energy from that job in anticipation of future job hunts.

As we'll see later, this step of the process had mixed results, which means that some of my approaches need to be refined further to really manifest the success I desired.

The Third Step: Undoing the Saboteur

Both my ex-wife and I had a tendency to sabotage ourselves just when it seems like we were getting what we really want. She had a tendency to worry a lot and thus projected the worst possible outcome on a situation. My sabotaging when it comes to wealth was much more insidious, because it's rather subtle. The sabotage was a tendency to believe that success could only be gained with lots of struggle. I was told this a lot by my mother, probably because she did have to struggle a lot in her life, but also because she discourages success when she sees other people manifesting it. I didn't realize until very recently that I actually believed that I had to struggle before I could succeed. It was only in the process of manifesting a move to Portland that I actually came face to face with this sabotaging pattern of behavior.

About a month before we were going to move, I suddenly experienced an onset of doubt about moving to Portland. I began to convince myself that maybe it wasn't such a good idea, that maybe I should give Seattle another chance (even though I knew that Seattle doesn't fit me). I realized I doubted myself, but I pegged it for potential moving jitters, even as I half-seriously considered just moving to a new place in Seattle and continuing to live there. Fortunately I was smart enough to realize that I needed to get a relatively objective opinion.

As it happened, at the end of April that year, Lupa and I were being flown out to Oberlin College to present workshops. My friend Maryam told me she'd be able to see me that day, and since she didn't live in Seattle or Portland, she had no vested interest in whether I stayed in one place or moved to another. I asked her if she would be willing to do a reading for me, and she graciously agreed. During this trip, I was also reading a book, *Secrets of the Millionaire Mind* by T. Harv Eker and between the Tarot reading and that book I came to fully realize how I was sabotaging myself by giving into the doubt I felt.

Maryam and I both do a style of Tarot reading which I would call freestyle reading. Instead of using set spreads for reading the cards, we randomly develop a spread for each situation. By doing this we avoid letting ourselves confuse the meaning of the cards with the meaning of the spread. Both she and I have noted that traditional spreads have associated meanings with the way the cards are set up, which can consequently confuse the actual reading. I shuffled the cards and created a V spread with a triangle in the middle of it. One branch of the V represented my choice to live in Seattle, and the other branch represented Portland.

The cards for Seattle had a lot of heat and fire imagery. The end result of them also indicated that I would have to put a universe's worth of effort into creating what I wanted. Any success I might find would involve dealing with lots of obstacles. Intriguingly enough, while doing this reading, I overheard one person ask where Taylor was and another mention that Taylor was sick (We were in a university building with students). There was a great amount of coincidence in that, which I consider a sign of the divine rapping me over the head to make sure I understood that Seattle never was, nor would be my home.

The cards for Portland had lots of water imagery and suggestions of refreshment and relaxation. They represented the path of least resistance toward the results I wanted. The cards also suggested that I would be delving even deeper into the internal journeys I was on. The result card was the woman of crystals, which has been a card I'd been using to represent myself in some of my magical workings. The overall card suggested synergy, that in each case an alignment of purpose and energy would manifest, but one approach would be much better than another.

The reading helped me realize that I had an important choice to make, and that choice wasn't so much about where I lived (though that was important too!), so much as it was about whether I wanted to continue living a life where I expected to overcome obstacles to achieve success, or whether I wanted to live a life where I took the path of least resistance and effort to achieve the greatest impact.

As I mentioned above, I was reading Eker's book at the time. Between the Tarot reading and his book I realized something very important. Some of the exercises in his book showed me how my attitudes toward finances were symptomatic of the attitude I had toward living life. I had always asked myself if I could handle failure, but in reading his book I realized that living life isn't about handling failure. People handle and live with failure every day. Failure is easy to live with. Each day people fail and yet each day people pick themselves up, dust off, and get back to living, or at least surviving.

So if I already lived with failure, what was the question I really had to ask? At first, I thought it was, "Can I handle success?" But I realized I already knew the answer to that question. I could, can and will always be able to risk being successful, because I've already been successful. This didn't mean I couldn't learn to handle greater degrees of success. We can all learn to handle greater degrees of success and I agree with Eker that people internally decide their own capacity for handling success. But the real question, the true secret to wealth of any kind, was I could risk being happy?

I have to admit that until fairly recently I've not lived a very happy life. I spent most of my twenties struggling toward happiness, keyword being struggled. So when I asked myself if I could risk being happy, my first reaction was, "No." I meditated on that answer, wanting to know why I felt this way. My meditation revealed that I had come expect that in order to be happy or be successful I had to struggle in life. I didn't like having that behavior pattern in me. I knew I needed to deconstruct it.

The Tarot reading I got from Maryam showed me how to deconstruct this behavior pattern. I could choose to continue living in Seattle and settle for a life of struggle in order to obtain success and happiness, or I could take the path of least resistance, and risk being happy without having to struggle. The choice was obvious. Any doubts I had about moving to Portland faded. I knew our move would be successful and that we would have jobs, a place to live, and a lot more happiness than we'd ever find in Seattle. And the land in Portland sung to me in a way that Seattle never had. So why ignore that call, why settle for less? I told Lupa the result of the Tarot reading and she agreed with me.

Step Four: Telling Lies to Make them into Reality

Once we'd decided to move to Portland, there was just one more problem to solve. I had to figure out how to quit my job. See, I really liked my job. In fact, it was the only thing I liked about Seattle. I worked with good people and I enjoyed the work I did, plus I had enough free time at work, occasionally to actually do my own work and my team lead didn't care as long as I kept producing the results he wanted. Not only that, but we'd finally gotten a second tech writer and he was thrilled to have two of us.

But my team lead did have one flaw in the sense that he took anyone leaving his group very personally and could make their lives hell for the last couple weeks. I love harmony and I didn't want to tell him I was leaving unless I could provide a really good reason for leaving. Telling him I was moving to Portland because Seattle didn't feel right to me just didn't seem like a reason that would work. I had to figure out a good reason to explain why we were moving. And I did.

I told him that my wife had gotten a full time job with a publishing company in Portland. It was a lie, but it worked…no politics, no drama, a very happy send off, and a bit of magic…because even though the words uttered were a lie at the time, I believed that words can shape reality and my belief was that my wife would get a job as an editor, if enough people believed what I told them. Belief is energy and if you can direct that energy you can manifest anything.

As another bit of word magic, I also wrote a couple articles and indicated that I would be living in Portland in May 2007. Set a belief in written word and you give it more impetus to spread...that was Burrough's approach to magic and one I've used to good effect. I figured if I set a definite date for when we'd live in Portland, it could only help the magic manifest what we needed.

Conclusion: The Process Manifests Results

As I mentioned above, both Lupa and I tended to worry. One of the principles in Eker's book was that people who had negative attitudes attracted negativity to them (2005). I'd seen this principle in both our lives a number of times. I'll admit that a big part of the problem with living in Seattle was my attitude. I attracted a lot of the negativity that I felt there (though not all of it...I do trust my intuition when it says this place doesn't want you here). I knew that even though we were both firm on living in Portland that we'd both need to help each other with the occasional bout of doubt and negativity that inevitably happens when you get ready to move and not everything is secure. I also knew that she and I had differing beliefs about security. She admitted she needed security. I could care less, because for me security was a delusion people tried to convince themselves was real. But I could respect her need for it, because I had needed it once as well, until the realities of graduate school stripped away the scales on my eyes.

We'd both done a lot of magic. After the trip to Oberlin was over, other than my daily prayers, I stopped doing the magic and let the process manifest the results (i.e. signs) we needed to have to know we were on the right track. And the results always came in at just the right time. Whenever either of us expressed doubt, within a day something would happen that confirmed we were on the right path. For example, we started looking for a place to live, but we just couldn't seem to find a place in the area we wanted to live. We'd remarked half-jokingly that it would be really cool if the people that lived about some friends moved out. Lo and behold, our friends told us that they were moving out and we began the process of securing the place we wanted to live in. When one of us expressed doubts about finding a job, an interview would be offered a day or so later.

Every time we needed confirmation, it came. Each result that manifested confirmed that the process was working. When we moved down to Portland everything pretty much fell into place. Some results indicated that the process needed to be refined, but overall I was pleased. We moved into the home we wanted, Lupa did get a job as an editor at a company, and I also landed a short term job. In fact, my job was the only fly in the ointment. While I'd gotten a job at the right time, it wasn't quite the job I had wanted. I had hoped for a shorter commute, health benefits, and much more stable work. Yet when I looked back on what I did, I realized I hadn't specified those needs in the prayers I'd recited or the related job magic. I had left the interpretation open to the magic and it gone down the route of least resistance, though not the best results. Instead of being discouraged I've already begun refining it for my next job hunt.

What we can learn from my mistake is that when magic doesn't work it's usually because of human error. By not being as specific as possible, I manifested what was easy to manifest, but not necessarily what was best.

Commentary

I wrote this article in 2008, and it aptly reflects a different understanding of wealth than I have now. I consider all of the workings that I described in this article to be an example of reactive wealth magic. I chose to do these workings because I was reacting to a situation I didn't like to be in. I resorted to some fairly questionable magical tactics that I likely wouldn't employ now. I achieved results, but the results were short term. The job I got was a two month contract and although it was extended to another two months, after that I was out of work for several more months.

It also took a lot of effort to pull this working off. I was able to tie together multiple magical workings and get the results I wanted for both myself and my ex-wife, up to and including not only jobs, but also a living situation we thought we wanted. But even though I did all of that work I still wasn't happy with the result. The truth is that I didn't know myself and what I wanted and while I am glad I moved to Portland (a wise choice all things considered) I hadn't addressed the underlying issues in my life that prompted the need to move until a few years and a divorce later.

In my opinion, wealth magic, or magic in general shouldn't have to be that complicated. You can make sure it isn't by taking the time to really understand what you want. You do that through meditation and also through honest communication with your partner. I wouldn't do this kind of wealth magic now and I wouldn't recommend it to anyone, but I thought I'd share it as an example of what I consider reactive wealth magic to be.

Bibliography

Alexander, Michelle (2012). *The new jim crow: Mass incarceration in the age of colorblindedness.* New York: The New Press.

Dominguez, Joe & Robin, Vicki. (1992). *Your money or your life: Transforming your relationship with money and achieving financial independence.* New York: Penguin Books.

Duhigg, Charles. (2012). *The power of habit: Why we do what we do and how to change it.* New York: Random House.

Eker, T. Harv. (2005). *Secrets of the millionaire mind: Mastering the inner game of wealth.* New York: HarperCollins Publishers, Inc.

Ellwood, Taylor. (2007). Inner Alchemy: energy work and the magic of the body. Stafford: Megalithica Books.

Ellwood, Taylor. (2012). *Magical identity: An exploration of space/time, neuroscience, and identity.* Stafford: Megalithica Books.

Fisher, Mark & Allen, Marc. (1997). *How to think like a millionaire.* Novato: New World Library.

Gardner, David, & Gardner, Tom. (2001). *You have more than you think: The foolish guide to personal finance.* New York: Simon & Schuster, Inc.

Kasser, Tim. (2006). "Materialism and Its Alternatives" (pp. 200-214). In Csikszentmihalyi & Csikszentmihalyi. *A life worth living: Contributions to positive psychology.* Oxford: Oxford University Press.

Kiyosaki, Robert T. (2000). *Rich dad, poor dad: What the rich teach their kids about money--That the poor and middle class do not!* New York: Warner Business Books.

Lee, Dave. (2011). *The wealth magick workbook: Or buddy can you spare a paradigm.* Runa-Raven Press.

Miller, Jason. (2012). *Financial sorcery: Magical strategies to create real and lasting wealth.* Pompton Plains: New Page Books.

Mierzwicki, Tony. (2008). *Graeco-Egyptian Magick.* Stafford: Immanion Press.

Schwartz, David J. (2007). *The magic of thinking big.* New York: Simon & Schuster, Inc.

Wattles, Wallace D. (2007). *The science of getting rich: Attracting financial success through creative thought.* Rochester: Destiny Books.

Recommended Reading

The following books (in addition to the ones mentioned above) are recommended reading for finances, business, and relationships. I've opted to include (for relationships) titles on subjects such as infidelity because I think that taking a proactive approach and reading about and discussing such topics with your partner(s) can help you have needed conversations that diffuse problems and allow you to build a wealthier and happier life of shared values and actions.

Finance

Smart Couples Finish Rich by David Bach
Dialogue Gap by Peter Nixon
In Good Times and Bad by M. Gary Neuman and Melisa Neuman

Business

Small Business Survival Book by Barbara Weltman and Jerry Silberman
The Power of Unpopular by Erika Napoletano
Growing your Business by Mark LeBlanc
Go for No! by Richard Fenton and Andrea Waltz
The E-myth Revisited by Michael Gerber
The Power of Why by C Richard Weylman
Networking Magic by Rick Frishman and Jill Lublin
From Good to Great by Jim Collins
Built to Last by Jim Collins
Great by Choice by Jim Collins
How the Mighty Fall and Why some Companies never give in by Jim Collins

Relationships

The Passionate Marriage by David Schnarch

Love and Awakening by John Welwood
Journey of the Heart by John Welwood
Perfect Love, Imperfect Relationships by John Welwood
Undefended Love by Jett Psaris and Marlena Lyons
After the Honeymoon by Daniel Wile
Transcending Post-Infidelity Stress Disorder by Dennis Ortman
After the Affair By Janis Abrahms Spring
Not 'Just Friends' by Shirley Glass

About Taylor Ellwood

Taylor Ellwood is the author of Magical Identity, Space/Time Magic, Inner Alchemy, Multi-Media Magic, and Pop Culture Magic Magic. He is also the Managing Editor of Immanion Press. He is also the founder and teacher of The Way of the Magician Mystery School You can find him on the web at the following:

http://www.magicalexperiments.com
http://www.twitter.com/magicexperiment
http://www.facebook.com/magicalexperiments

The Way of the Magician Mystery School

The Way of the Magician is a Mystery School that I have developed to formalize and improve on the work that I have written about in my books. It is a fusion of Western magical practices and Eastern mystical practices, with an emphasis on creating a balanced approach to doing internal work for spiritual and personal growth, while also doing practical workings to solve problems and improve the quality of your life. The Way of the Magician is designed to supplement and enhance any spiritual work you are doing in other magical traditions while still presenting a unique perspective and approach to magical work.

What makes the Way of the Magician Mystery School unique is the integration of modern disciplines and cultural studies into your spiritual work. I think it is important for magic, as a discipline and spiritual practice, to evolve with the times, and part of this is done by exploring how other disciplines such as neuroscience, rhetoric, literacy, etc. can be meaningfully applied to spiritual practices.

If you would like to learn more about available classes at The Way of the Magician Mystery School, please visit http://www.magicalexperiments.com/way-of-the-magician/

CPSIA information can be obtained
at www.ICGtesting.com
Printed in the USA
FSOW01n2242090316
17759FS